silence

SILENCE

making the journey to inner quiet

Barbara Erakko Taylor

Innisfree
Press, Inc.

A call to the
deep heart's core

Innisfree Press, Inc.
136 Roumfort Road
Philadelphia, PA 19119-1632

Cover photograph by Pam Taylor: El Convento in Arequipa, Peru
Interior photographs by Barbara Erakko Taylor

Library of Congress Cataloging-in-Publication Data
Taylor, Barbara Erakko, date.
      Silence : making the journey to inner quiet /
   by Barbara Erakko Taylor
          p.   cm.
      ISBN 1-880913-21-6
      1. Silence.   2. Taylor, Barbara Erakko, date.
   3. Spiritual biography—United States.   I. Title.
   BJ1499.S5E73   1997
   291.4'46'092—dc21
   [B]   97-11593

   Grateful acknowledgment is made to the following for permission
to reprint copyrighted material:
   From *The Poems of St. John of the Cross*, copyright © 1972 by Willis
Barnstone. Used by permission of New Directions Publishing Corporation.
   From *The Collected Works of St. John of the Cross* (Revised Edition),
translated by Kieran Cavanaugh and Otiliro Rodriguez, copyright © 1991
by The Washington Province of Discalced Carmelite Friars, Inc., published
by I.C.S. Publications, Washington, D.C. Used by permission of Kieran
Cavanaugh.

Belief in yourself can go a long way,
but not long enough
without belief from others.
— my daughter, Lisa Taylor

In thanksgiving for the belief from others:

Elsie Norlund Nurmi
for giving me life and a mother's love

Sr. Anita Schuman, O.C.D.
for guiding me safely into the world of silence

Sandra Nurmi Hall
for listening, laughing, and loving me since I was born

Bill Morris Taylor
for loving me before, during, and after

SILENCE

making the journey to inner quiet

But I have stilled and quieted my soul,
like a weaned child with its mother,
like a weaned child is my soul within me.

— Psalm 131:2, New International Version

contents

PART I: MEETING SILENCE

One dark night,
fired with love's urgent longings
— ah, the sheer grace! —
I went out unseen,
my house being now all stilled.
— "Dark Night," St. John of the Cross

PART II: STRUGGLING WITH SILENCE

Why, since you wounded
this heart, don't you heal it?
And why, since you stole it from me,
do you leave it so,
and fail to carry off what you have stolen?
— "Spiritual Canticle," St. John of the Cross

PART III: BUILDING SILENCE INTO A LIFESTYLE

She lived in solitude,
in solitude she made her nest
and all alone her lover
led her in solitude,
wounded in solitude by love.
— "Spiritual Canticle," St. John of the Cross

PART IV: LIVING IN SILENCE

The night of total calm
before the rising winds of dawn,
the music of a silence,
the sounding solitude,
the supper that renews our love.
— "Spiritual Canticle," St. John of the Cross

EPILOGUE

In deepest solitude
I found the narrow way:
a secret giving such release
that I was stunned and stammering
rising above all science.
— "I Came into the Unknowing," St. John of the Cross

prologue

Silence.

A word that evokes scary images of aloneness, of vulnerability, of having to face one's inner world. We say we want a deeper spiritual life, yet we deny it by avoiding perhaps one of the most crucial elements — silence. We are afraid of it. In our media-drenched culture, silence is intimidating.

A typical day in the life of an American begins with the TV flicked on to the morning news and weather. Our drive to work is soothed by music or the talk-jock of our favorite radio station. At work, we immerse ourselves in a tightly packed day of meetings, deadlines, and phone calls. We unwind on the way home with our favorite tape, CD, or radio station, and end our day with more TV, family talk, music, or a video.

The presence of noise is much more pervasive than at first glance. In the past, one of the major ways we encountered silence was by puttering around the home: washing, cleaning, repairing. Today, the household vibrates with noise: we wash dishes by machine, we vacuum by machine, we mow by machine, we even rake leaves by machine. We have lost our contact with ordinary, everyday silence. It has become a stranger. Our yearning for "something more" in our spiritual life grows, yet our lack of silence stands as a formidable roadblock. We know that in order to pray, we need to quiet ourselves, yet that is the very thing we fear most.

In the poem "The Hound of Heaven," written by Francis Thompson more than one hundred years ago, a man flees down the labyrinth of life escaping the pursuing hound only in the end to give up, exhausted, and find that all along it was God who was the pursuing hound.

For me, silence has been the pursuer. I ran from it down the corridor of my career, marriage and children, past blaring televisions and car radios. I dodged it by turning on churning dishwashers, standing under hissing water-jet showers, sucking up dirt with high-powered vacuum cleaners. And when all else failed, I opened a book, lest silence find me alone and vulnerable.

Who — or what — was silence that I feared it so much?

When silence finally breached my almost impenetrable defenses, I was chief designer for an automated information system destined for installation at the White House Executive Office. I worked fifty to sixty hours a week, managed a staff of fourteen, and reported to the senior vice-president of an aggressive and growing computer firm.

Then one night my husband almost died. Only thirty-seven years old, his heart became erratic. For the next five days, he hovered between life and death.

I tried to block the real possibility of his impending death from my mind. It was my most heroic and determined battle against silence. If I immersed myself in the sounds of life, I rationalized, perhaps the sound of my husband's heart would keep ticking. I turned on radios, televisions. I called people on the phone. I couldn't stand the silence of a hospital waiting room at 5:00 A.M.

I fought silence until I could fight no longer. Driving home alone and afraid from the hospital on a bleak, rain-cold night, I lost. No music could console me. I turned off the radio, and for the first time in my adult life, met silence.

Two days later, my husband turned the corner from death back to life. He slowly recovered and life resumed.

But I was not able to forget the night I left the radio disk jockey behind for the silence of tires rolling on a wet, cold, asphalt-empty highway. I began to quiet my world — a journey that has now lasted two decades.

When Bill came home, I turned the radio and television off. I turned the dishwasher off. I began to listen to myself passing through time — hearing the comforting chop of a vegetable knife on a wood board, the soft-sound scraping of a wood spatula against a cast iron skillet, the broom sweeping on wood floors.

Silence, I realized in the passing months, was more than turning off appliances. It was stilling the inner chaos of my body as well. For years, I had jump-started my day by drinking coffee. My typical office lunch had been cheese slices on dry crackers. Snacks were cookies and more coffee. Dinner was wine, meat, and a frozen vegetable. I'd get a rush from food. I'd talk fast, walk fast, work fast, and then fall into a deep slump hours later only to repeat the cycle. Now I began to listen to my body. I ate gentler foods. Rice. Beans. Vegetables.

At first, silence was no more than the tick-tick-tick of a clock on a shelf, the sound of wind blowing or acorns dropping on the roof. Then I met the silence of prayer when time is forgotten, the acorn is lost, and at last solitude could speak and make love to me.

Gradually, in very physical ways, I quieted my house, both inner and outer.

Then my husband and I decided to adopt two Korean sisters.

~

The noisy, demanding entry of a two- and four-year-old into our lives catapulted me out of the equilibrium I had created. In my efforts to parent these two Korean-speaking dynamos, I realized that, without silence, I would lose my confidence to enter this instant motherhood. Desperation drove me deeper into the strange world of silence.

When we took our newly adopted children to a mountain campground, I met a tiny, saffron-robed Buddhist monk who guided me into meditation. He struck a deep-throated brass gong, and his baritoned voice washed over the early morning dawn. Ironically, it was the sound of ancient monastic chants that opened the way ever deeper into the vast virgin cavern of silence.

I found myself overcome with an almost erotic longing for such deep stillness. Silence had seduced me. I sank deeper and deeper into prayer, wrapped in its honeymooned embrace. I thought my love for silence would last forever.

I thought right — and wrong.

~

One day I stood quietly gazing through our sliding glass doors. The first signs of Spring were beginning along the creek, the green skunk cabbage leaves thrusting up through the earth. It was a windless day, and without thinking, I found myself slipping into a silent world. Then something overcame me.

Whereas silence had been a visitor, a friend with whom I communed when I chose, now silence slipped into the core of my being. Without my knowing, without even my conscious consent, silence entered me in a way a spouse penetrates his espoused. I realized with a shock that this seeking of silence had led to consummation. I was consumed. I was wed — in a way that had no guests, no celebration, no fanfare or music, and no witness. Except my heart.

While outwardly I talked as much as ever and made every effort to remain connected with my daily affairs, inwardly I struggled to re-orient myself. Whereas, before, I would often be overcome by silence, drinking in great drafts of it, now I was confused by it.

It became unbearable to watch television. I could not read a book. If I tried, I kept reading the same line over and over again, unable to comprehend the words. This period lasted for several months. Everything, it seemed, filtered through silence, without which nothing in my life had meaning. I was enthralled by the depths to which silence was carrying me — and scared.

Distressed that I could not find the silence I once knew, I could no longer quiet myself. No prayer, no mantra, no word or breathing technique stilled the frantic tangle of thoughts racing through my mind. Sitting quietly was no longer easy. No longer desirable. I wanted to flee, yet I had loved too much and been loved too much to abandon this mysterious silent lover.

I began to seek silence and could not find it anywhere. In the crowded mall, on the Summer boardwalk, in the loneliness of a hotel room, I yearned for, and sought, silence. But there was nothing of what I had remembered. It was gone.

Silence had abandoned me.

I entered into a period of not knowing. I felt myself being inexplicably drawn to a confusing answer — an answer to the age-old question I had not even asked: "Who do you say I am?"

Initially I answered, "Not God. Surely, not that."

~

My husband could not understand me nor the silence that enveloped me. That, and other difficulties, led us into therapy and me into spiritual direction. Eight years later we painfully agreed to separate, and two years after that, the marriage ended.

As I faced and grieved the loss of my marriage, silence slowly returned. Not physical silence but interior silence — the peace that passes all understanding. It returned to usher me into a life that had been prepared for me a long time ago — a life of solitude.

In the silence of the days and nights, I was quieted not by force but by responding to the silent call of Love. I sought the mystery of God. I began to know silence as a friend: in the still, cold morning; in each single blooming flower; in the quiet walk up the street; in the darkening night. Everywhere I met silence.

I began to call it the unfinished symphony. I know silence so well now, it is hard to remember why I feared it so much. Perhaps I was terrified of the cacophony of my own humanity — the noise of hurts and wounds, of heartaches and loss. Perhaps that was my symphony — one filled with anger and fear — and yet also with frail hope and love.

~

The story is far from over. I sometimes still fear and often flee silence. Those who know me know that I literally leap into life, sometimes, even now, flinging myself into it almost desperately to avoid solitude. Yet I exhaust myself quickly — more quickly with each passing year — and return to my silent home, my solitary way.

I stand, perhaps, on the edge of being a hermit. Hermits have no coda, no definition, no theology. They simply are the living embodiments of silence. As such, they are an enigma to society. And they themselves rarely claim any special enlightenment, any mystical spirituality. What they would probably say is, "I love silence." That is all.

Perhaps that is enough.

making the journey to inner quiet

PART I: MEETING SILENCE

One dark night,
fired with love's urgent longings
— ah, the sheer grace! —
I went out unseen,
my house being now all stilled.

— "Dark Night," St. John of the Cross

SILENCE

silent beginnings

*I*t is late, about 10:00 P.M. I am alone, driving down the streets of inner city Baltimore. Filled with anxious dread, I flick on the radio. It is set to light rock. An upbeat melody. A catchy dance tune.

Three miles away, my husband lies dying.

Two days earlier, he had complained about feeling sick. The sulfa drugs for flu the doctor had prescribed weren't working. "Just get some rest," I had told him. "You'll be fine. The drugs just haven't kicked in yet."

That night, I curled myself around his lanky body. It was another cold March night. We both fell asleep.

"Barbara! I don't feel good."

I reached out to touch him. Thud. I heard his body fall onto the bedroom floor.

From that moment time, as I knew it, stopped. It lay hidden in some foreign place I couldn't remember or find.

The next instant I remember was pressing my hand against Bill's neck, searching for a pulse. He opened his eyes. He looked scared.

"I'm calling an ambulance!" I said, racing for the phone.

"No," Bill weakly insisted. "Call Pete."

"ANSWER IT, PETE. PICK UP THE PHONE," I silently urged my brother-in-law as I frantically dialed his number.

"Hello?" I heard Pete's deep gravely voice yawn into the receiver.

"Pete, Bill's sick. He needs to go to a hospital right away. I don't think he can walk. I need your help. I don't think the ambulance can find our house." We lived on a secluded, unmarked road at the end of a concealed gravel driveway.

I struggled to dress Bill. He slumped in my arms. I kept working quickly. Socks, shoes. Five minutes later, I heard the door open.

It was 2:00 A.M. Pete and I half-carried Bill to the car. I sat in the back seat while Pete raced down the deserted road.

"He's passing out, Barbara," Pete said seeing Bill's body slump.

"Stay awake," I begged, slapping Bill's cheeks. Pete pushed harder on the gas pedal, flinging us through the dark night.

~

"I don't know what's going on," the cardiologist said, starting to unroll a long strip of paper. "See here — that's fibrillation." Jabbing another section, "That's a massive heart attack. Here, there's no heart beat at all. Here, it's normal." He looked at me with quiet brown eyes. "I don't know what's happening. We can try to get him to Johns Hopkins Hospital. They have some of the best heart specialists in the world. But he might die on the way. Or we can keep him here. What do you want to do?"

"Take him to Hopkins," I said in a small terrified voice.

~

"Mrs. Taylor?"

I jumped up as a white-coated, older man walked over to me. Three hours had passed with no news about my husband. With a hand motion, the doctor gestured for me to sit.

"Your husband has had a rough night. He was Code Blue twice. We almost lost him. He's stable now, so you can see him for a few minutes. We've got some specialists scheduled to look in on him this morning."

I walked through partially drawn curtains into a small vestibule. Bill's eyes were closed. He looked pale and unreal, tied to what seemed like a million machines. I looked at the one that seemed to be monitoring his heart. The early morning silence unnerved me. No carts rolling down the hall. No nurses chattering. Suddenly a high pierced alarm went off in the room. *My God, he's DYING.* I felt the air being sucked out of me. I waited for the sound of pounding footsteps, of doctors rushing in. But nothing happened. The alarm stopped. I watched the staccato green spikes once again inch their way across the monitor. I heard a beep from a machine in another vestibule. Occasionally an alarm punctured the silence.

Human activity was not measured by the normal signs of life, but by the sound — or silence — of machines.

~

"Mrs. Taylor?"

It was now three days later. The doctor came in, his eyes

scanning the waiting room for me. In the corridor, I heard a cart clattering along the floor. Two women laughing. In the waiting room, hushed conversations. We knew each other's stories — whose husband had had a heart attack, whose daughter had a genetic heart defect, who was expected to die. The doctors came in, their normal voices unnaturally amplified in our hushed world. Their matter-of-fact words ripping hope apart or knitting it together.

Now it was my turn. Everyone fell silent.

"We're stopping all treatment. Mr. Taylor's not responding. He's getting worse." Quickly the doctor summarized all the treatments they'd tried so far. I already knew what he was now officially telling me: each had been disastrous. Bill was hanging by a thread, and no one seemed to know how to snatch him to safety.

"We'll continue to monitor him." By that, I knew they could Code Blue him in an instant and shock him back into life. That was the best they could do.

～

I turn left onto Greene Street heading south. The radio is crooning Stevie Wonder, "You are the sunshine of my life."

In the eerily silent city streets, with my husband fighting for his life in a white-walled cubicle, I can't handle love — the hope, life, promise of it. I want to tear the sing-song notes out of the air.

I spin the radio dial, sending the needle flying to the right, slowing down where I think the classical music crowd hangs out on the air waves. I am always a little leery of classical music. It seems to creep past all my barriers, leaving me as defenseless against its funereal fugues as its rhapsodic passions.

On this bleak March night, the station is broadcasting a

depressing groan of organ music, its haunting sound commingling with the terror held at bay in the bowels of my belly. *How could you write this?* I scream silent fury at the composer, rage overwhelming me. I choke back a cry, blindly driving down the potholed, inner-city road.

I am still thirty minutes from home. *Easy listening,* I decide. *That's what I need. Something mindless, something soothing.* My fingers slowly twist the dial, searching for the melodic old-time tunes that will ease this terrible ache, this gnawing fear inside me.

"What the world needs now is love, sweet love," a sugary sweet voice mouths into the car.

Stop! STOP! I beat the steering wheel in rage.

If I can just hold on, I tell myself, *I can make this nightmare go away.*

All my life I have *controlled* — my ideas, my needs, my work, my dreams. *Surely there must be some way I can WILL Bill to live,* I desperately think.

It is my way of dealing with stress: try harder, do more. Perhaps what I really fear is the silence of non-doing.

It is safer to let allthingsruntogether.

~

I roll down the almost-empty highway, the music eating up the silence I don't want to be in, the silence I am terrified of. I cover up the silence, smothering it with sound in the frantic, animal-like hope that if the noise is loud enough or soothing enough or happy enough, I won't have to face the pain. Bill is only thirty-seven. I am thirty-two. But now our ages — like time itself — float in a strange timelessness. Tonight, tomorrow, I might be a widow. He might be dead.

I look at the radio. There are no more channels to try.

I turn it off.

For the first time in my adult life, I meet silence face-to-face.

~

The road is almost deserted. The blower softly fans my legs with warm air. Beneath a starless sky, evening slowly wraps itself around me. I feel my anguish-torn body sink into it, deeper and deeper. Everything in me aches: my thought-racing mind, my bone-weary body. Fear is eating chunks of my flesh.

During those first few days of Bill's hospitalization, I had fought back against all this: With orderly thoughts. With pajamas and a toothbrush for Bill, should he ever need it. With telephone calls to my mother and father to come home. With music, television — anything to distract me.

Now, through sheer exhaustion, I have fallen into silence.

Strange, I know this silence like some ancient, long-forgotten memory . . . of myself as a child "wasting" time on a swing in the park . . . lying on my parents' chaise lounge in the screened porch watching wrens flit into their nesting box . . . taking lazy walks to the library where even the smell of books seemed erotic.

How had I forgotten all of that?

As I quietly roll through the darkness, my thoughts begin to float. Untrapped, unfettered, they begin to expand like butterflies emerging from a tight-spun cocoon. They stand damp and uncertain on the edge of their chrysalis, wondering what to do.

One thought after another dries its unbound wings, slowly testing them, opening them to the still night air. And just as slowly, they begin to spread their wings. Perhaps I am too tired to fight them any longer.

Some thoughts taunt me. Like black-and-gray winged creatures, they murmur, *He might die. He might die.* Others sicken me with their putrid wings of blame: *It's your fault. You should have realized this sickness was different.*

Strangely, the last thought to touch my exhausted consciousness is as quiet and unassuming as a single butterfly with pure white wings. It lingers, content to comfort me with a tiny flutter of hope: *Perhaps he will live.*

water

*B*ill and I snuggle deeper into our down sleeping bags, listening to the icy rain pelt the outside of our tent. The air has that raw, early Spring cut to it. We crawl out the next morning, carefully avoiding the puddled water on the plastic sheet beneath our tent.

Unpacking breakfast fixings, we review the passage of the night, the weather, the plans for the day. But our words are sparse, quiet sounds not jarring the stillness of dawn. We huddle over the topographic map. Today, we plan to hike eleven miles.

After three weeks in the hospital and three months at home, Bill has now returned to work. Only the cardiologist knows that his heart has a right bundle branch blockage. He has made a full recovery except for the loss of certain nerves used to trigger his heart beat. His life expectancy is normal, but it takes him longer now to climb steep trails.

Today as we heave on our backpacks and step onto the rocky trail, a comfortable silence falls between us. Soon we are each lost in our thoughts, our strides matched by years of walking up and down trails together. We pass through a grove of hemlocks and pines. The wind has torn the leeward branches from them. In the quiet stillness of morning, they look like bonsai-pruned gnomes.

I stoop to touch a silvery patch of dew-glistened moss and then quicken my step to catch up. The trails are faint, often as thin as a deer's hoof across granite, and it is relaxing to follow Bill's backpack.

Only the sound of our breath and the rhythmic crunch of our boots connect us to each other in the cool morning silence of the day. Occasionally, the screech of a hawk or the song of a bird ripples across the stillness and then disappears.

We never ask each other what time it is, or how far we have hiked. The hours, like our cadenced breath, eddy out soundlessly beneath the rising sun.

Reaching the top of the hill, the trail splays into two unmarked footways. Bill and I stop to consult the map. Then we resume our silent journey.

I feel the boundaries of my life — the entrapments of hectic work schedules, meetings, deadlines — slip soundlessly away. Like clothes that are too heavy to wear on a hot day, I slowly shed each problem weighing me down: The sticky design problem I can't solve. The staff person I am irritated with. The speech I haven't written. The proposal that is due.

I always find comfort in the silence of nature — and even more so when I am with a quiet companion.

We crest a ridge. The trail begins a gradual descent into a vast, bowl-shaped meadow, an emerald-grassed garden that flourishes beneath the sweeping winds overhead. Beaver ponds dot the landscape. Scores of sun-scorched tree trunks give mute testimony to the dark-furred victors.

~

"I think we've lost the trail," Bill breaks the silence, reaching for his map. "Do you see a cairn?"

Slowly I scan the horizon with the binoculars. "No," I say, giving up.

Bill flips open his compass. After a few minutes, he picks up the binoculars.

"There it is," he says, pointing to a spot several hundred yards away, a small gray pyramid of rocks at the end of a grove of hemlock trees.

"Good," I respond hungrily, "Let's eat lunch."

It is 1:00 P.M. My feet are bruised after hours of stumbling along a rocky trail. Seeing Bill put down his pack, I shrug mine off and unlace my boots.

I gingerly walk barefoot to the small mountain stream winding its way through the meadow and step into its icy waters, shivering with cold delight. The water turns my feet red with cold. I feel numbness setting in and wiggle my toes, reluctant to get out.

Bill sits on a beaver-felled tree, its sun-dried wood now white with age. I dry my feet on my flannel shirt and make my way over to the log. Our lunch today is sardines, crackers, and an apple.

I dip my fingers into the can, pulling out a greasy sardine. As my hunger pains begin to subside, I eat slower and slower, and gaze with delight into this tiny, alpine-like world.

The crisp, rain-washed air has polished the cloudless blue sky to a crystalline sheen. The marsh meadow grass glimmers beneath the sun, leaving a wet-willowy green brilliance. The clear, brown water of the beavers' home is stirred with sun-silver-stroked reflections. I return to the stream to watch the water wind through the meadow.

Knowing Bill is close by allows me to enjoy the awesomeness of deserted wilderness. It has taken me time to learn to appreciate the undomesticated beauty of raging mountain streams to be crossed on precariously narrow logs or wet rocks . . . ill-marked trails traversed on moonless nights . . . campsites where poisonous spiders crawl. All of my senses used to be attuned to survival, with precious little attention left to enjoy the silence of a wilderness setting.

Until I learned, over the years, to trust Bill.

An experienced hiker, unflappable in emergencies, Bill gradually weaned me from my fear. He always got me home safely. After decades of merging our rhythms into one another, now I hardly give a second thought to potential danger. On this day, I sink with intoxicated joy into the thrill of the beaver meadow.

I begin to trace the mountain stream's path with my eye across the valley. It carries its rippling peat-moss water over the rocks as carefree as a child tumbling down grass in delight.

I walk to the water's edge and place my hands palm down beneath the skin of the mountain stream. The water slowly reveals a limpid beauty beneath its sinuous shimmer, like a woman relishing her nakedness. It rolls over and over and over me, trailing its sequinned charm across my flesh.

I take out my hands and watch as she flows out of sight.

～

"We'd better go," Bill calls. I leave my watery musing, stand up, and stretch. The burdens of a hectic life feel far, far away. Bill hoists the pack onto my back. I groan. The straps bearing seventeen pounds of equipment bite into my shoulders.

We head for the cairn.

~

Sometimes if the grass in our yard shimmers a certain way, I remember that day, walking through the silence behind Bill, stopping for lunch by the beaver ponds. I close my eyes and watch the stream meander through that mountain meadow once again, her topaz, sun-sequinned beauty rushing over my hands.

I can pour my thoughts, my weariness, my confusion into those waters. The banks broaden and deepen. The water rolls over them like a mother burbling sounds of love to her tiny infant child, hushing it to sleep with her soft, lulling voice. I feel my heart sink deep into my soul. A silent river of joy runs through me.

the glacier

Standing beside my husband, looking up at Mt. Blanc towering over us, I am not sure I want to go up its precipitous granite walls — even in a cable car.

I watch the red-and-white car, comfortingly large in its town terminal, slowly swing out of its berthing place. The people inside seem insignificant — fragile voyagers on a tenuously thin cable of time — compared to the ageless eternity of the mountain.

Soon, it is no more than a red speck, a single car swinging beneath a single wired thread like a spider on a gossamered line.

I am mesmerized, unable to turn away my gaze — and afraid.

~

A year has passed since Bill's hospitalization. While we talk about children, neither of us is quite ready. I am wrapped up in my career; Bill feels uncertain about his health. Putting long-range plans aside, we decide to vacation in Europe.

Fifteen years ago, after I graduated from college and Bill completed his Army duty, we had withdrawn our entire life savings and gone camping. On a shoestring budget, we traveled Scandinavia, several Communist countries, and Europe for three carefree months. Then we came home, found jobs, and eked out two weeks of vacation a year like greedy misers. Now we wanted to return to Switzerland and France to hike in the alpine foothills. We packed our bags and camping gear, and booked a charter flight.

In a rare splurge from our econo-camper's budget, we purchase tickets up Mt. Blanc. The first ticket takes us up, in two stages, to the top of the cable run up Mt. Blanc. The final thirty-minute run will carry us six kilometers across a faceless glacier into Italy.

We step into the line of chattering, camera-carrying tourists. As the cable car looms into view, I see the faces of the people inside laughing, smiling, stooping to pick up their gear. They jostle out one side as we surge into the other, tracking our wet boots onto the muddy floor.

I listen to the motor in the terminal as we slowly swing out of our portal. Soon we are airborne, rapidly gaining altitude above the village of Chamonix. People are excitedly pointing to things. Bill is snapping pictures. I force my anxiety down and look out, determined to open myself to the imposing silence of this ice cold mountain, its gray stone face now giving way to a pure white covering of snow.

We reach the first debarkation point. The next car is one-sixth the size of the first. Bill hands me a down vest and a yellow windbreaker. I put them on and begin anxiously to study our second ascent. It is considerably steeper. The cable looks like a dangling rope tossed down the side of the mountain. Rescue attempts seem impossible.

We step into the car and the door slides shut. Soon we are crawling up the side of the mountain face. I watch intently as we near the top. Fifty feet, twenty feet, clunk. We are docked. I sigh with relief, step out, and gasp. Spread below me, like meringue frozen in time, lie uncountable peaks buried beneath the crushing weight of snow.

The wind swirls violently around us. We grip the guard rails. The traverse from here to Italy is closed, and I am relieved. I have seen as much of this silent, foreboding world as I want to see. I am ready to go back to the safety of quaint Chamonix.

Then the announcement comes: "The car to Italy is open."

I don't want to go. But it's too late. Bill grabs my arm and hurries me forward. The tiny door swings open; the attendant urges us in. The door slams shut, the motor cranks, and we swing out — over a silence bounded by moon-barren ice beneath and an over-cast sky above. It is an eerie silence.

I look down. A crevasse, perhaps decades old, has ripped the massive landscape in two — evidence of shifting blocks of granite grinding and scraping along this frozen sea.

The car sways back and forth. If it had been a hammock beneath the warm summered leaves of an ancient tree, I might have been lulled to sleep by its gentle rocking motion. But sus-pended several hundred feet above ice on a wire, I tighten up in mindless terror, my hands gripping my pack.

~

"Bill," I whisper. "It's stopped moving."

Our car has lurched to an abrupt halt. We are suspended over a tomb of ice.

"What's wrong?" I hear my voice sounding tight, terrified.

"I don't know," Bill answers.

There is no sound. Nothing.

This is the silence of DEATH. I silently shudder at the thought: *The ears hear no more. The eyes see no more. The hands touch no more.* It is an inhuman silence. The glacier gazes with cataracted eyes of ice into silence. I gaze into it with terror so intense even breath seems to stop, suspended, frozen in fear over the icy sea, unable to find its way to my lungs.

Minutes pass, the silent movement of the hands on my battered watch the only thing to assure me that I have life. I feel brutally held by this cold, indifferent, and frightening silence.

Suspended over the massive, slow-rivered glacier, I feel a tiny hint of the long battle ahead. Do I want to know only my definition of silence — a sweet, friendly, nurturing silence? Or do I want to know SILENCE?

Clunk. The car jerks into motion.

The ice goes on. And on. And on.

I don't have an answer. Yet.

the clock

*C*areful not to wake my husband, I quietly unzip my sleeping bag, edging my way off the wooden bunk in the tiny cabin. Outside, night has not yet yielded to dawn. It is 5:30 A.M., a cool May day in 1982. Over the last four years after my husband's near death, my life has gradually returned to normal — except that I have never turned on the car radio again. And over time, I have quieted my house. I now wash dishes by hand, preferring to watch the birds outside the window than hear the raucous sound of the dishwasher. I have changed my diet. No caffeine. Less meat. No sugar. Quieter food. I am less hyped up, less super-charged. But other than that, I have returned to my long hours and aggressive lifestyle.

I have just completed the installation of an information system for the Carter administration. Several federal agencies and some Fortune 500 companies are interested in the software. I travel nationally as a speaker and make my first international trip as a consultant.

If I think about silence at all, it is as a source of momentary relaxation, not as a way of life. It is the pause that refreshes — so I can pounce on the next project.

But for all my career successes and triumphs, I feel let down.

One day as I sit in my twelfth floor office looking out the window, I wonder about the meaning of my life. *What will my gravestone say?* I muse. *That she designed twenty-eight information systems?*

That is the day I begin to think about children.

~

I flip on the flashlight, shading its light with my hand, and look at our two sleeping daughters.

Daughters. A new word for us. Two sisters, adopted from Korea only weeks ago. Their black-tousled hair spreads out upon the pillow. Four-year-old Kendra, her thumb in her mouth, clutches a blue blouse in her hand, the one she wore in Korea. Lisa, two years younger, looks like a sleeping rag doll, arms and legs sprawling in all directions.

Five weeks ago, Bill and I traveled halfway around the world to pick up our children. They came into our lives like two high-powered explosions of energy. I was in love — and in shock. As much as I wanted them, they shattered my orderly world. I was suddenly faced with two miniature human beings who wanted to be held, played with, and fed — for a grueling sixteen-hour workday. And they didn't speak any English.

Now, we are taking our first vacation together in the Berkshire mountains. The camp offers vegetarian meals, children's activities, and alternate lifestyle courses for adults.

Shivering, I pull on my sweatshirt and pants, lace my shoes, and slip out the cabin door. I see other campers move like ghosts across the dew-drenched grass toward a dimly lit building.

Inside, fifty, perhaps sixty, people, mostly in their twenties and thirties, sit Indian-style on the bare wood floor. In front of us a tiny man, barely five feet, quietly moves around in a saffron orange robe. I gawk at his clean-shaven head and wonder if I've been right in giving up an extra hour of sleep. Do I really want to know about Buddhist prayer?

I yawn.

At 6:00 A.M., he begins talking: the origin of Buddhism; how it is practiced in Japan; the main tenets. I stifle another yawn. "I don't think you will become Buddhists," he says with a quiet smile on his face. "You have been born into a Judeo-Christian country. You have chosen this place and time. Your spiritual journey is here in this culture. Very few of you will be called to follow Buddhism."

What a strange statement, I think, my sleepy attention returning to the tiny Reverend Tanaka.

"Please experience my way of prayer," he invitingly suggests. "Perhaps it will help you on your own spiritual journey."

I have no spiritual journey, I reflect. *I am here because it is the only class I can take before the children wake up. The only time I have to be by myself.*

He asks us to get into a comfortable position for prayer. I can't find any, my legs already aching, my buttocks growing numb.

G-o-n-g. He strikes the ancient, bronze-metaled mother of sound. Clear, deep waves of its tone-warming resonance wash over us. He begins to intone ancient chants, like the low note on a cello, a solitary string reverberating. We join in, our chest cavities becoming human accompaniment. On and on it goes, up and down, cadences I have never heard before, each vibration loosening something deep inside me. I get this strange sensation of coming home to a friend. Like the night I first turned off the car radio.

Time passes. G-o-n-g. The sound washes over us again. The meditation is over.

Slowly we stand up, massaging aching, tingling limbs, and slip away.

Bill yawns and turns over to look at me as I slip back into the cabin. My eyes slowly adjust to the dark interior.

"Did you like it?" he murmurs, half asleep.

"I don't know," I answer.

~

Every morning for the next six days, I say to myself, *I'm not going. I'm too tired. This is too strange.* But then 5:30 comes, and I find myself struggling into my sweatshirt and pants. I doubt it is the prayer that draws me. More likely, it is the time to be alone.

Alone.

Swamped by the demands of two children, I wonder if I will ever be alone again. Overwhelmed with the children's needs, I have virtually stopped eating. The children eat four bowls of rice at a sitting; I eat one cup a day. I am losing weight, pound by pound, as I struggle into parenthood.

It is not until years later that I understand how traumatic that severing of my time to think, to create, is — a need buried beneath an avalanche of the mindless tasks and routines required to raise a child.

~

"Go see Bo In Lee," my new vacation friends insist. "He's like a psychologist, and he's Korean, like your children. He will help you. He's very wise."

Kendra, our active extrovert, runs all day from Bill to me, laughing, jumping, back and forth, back and forth, burbling in Korean, tugging on our hands to show us new things. Lisa clings to me and screams whenever I put her down. From dawn to dusk every day, I shift her diaper-soggy weight from one arm to the other. Exhausted, confused, uncertain about mothering, I make an appointment. *Surely he can advise me. This isn't a medical problem; it's emotional. I'm overwhelmed.*

~

I step into the cabin reserved for Bo In Lee's consultations. A square-built man, slender but solid in appearance with thick, black hair and intelligent eyes, sits on a wooden chair behind a fold-out table. I take the only other seat, opposite him. He smiles, takes my hand, and turns it over.

"Look," he says, pointing to a line running down the middle of my palm. "You have a strong spiritual line. Very strong. You must begin your spiritual journey. Now."

This is a mistake, I think, *coming to see him. I don't want my hand read.* If politeness hadn't been ingrained in me, I would have jerked my hand away.

What a strange emphasis: "*Now.*"

For fifteen years I have not set foot in a church. The last time was May 19, 1967 — the day I got married.

~

I don't remember Bo In Lee's advice about the children, but he promises to look at them sometime during the week. Bill remembers him stopping one evening at our table. I am too exhausted to remember. Lee apparently gazed for a long intent moment at each of our children's faces and then quietly talked to Bill.

At the end of the week, I sit for the last time with the Reverend Tanaka. There are only eleven of us left. We chant around the chloroform-treated swimming pool, the safety-roughed cement grinding into our ankle bones as we intone the almost-familiar chants. He ends by saying, "If you would like to continue, I will give you a copy of the chants we have used."

I take a stapled set of mimeographed sheets and say thank-you-and-good-bye to the little man.

~

Six months go by. Things begin to settle down. Kendra is speaking broken English instead of Korean. We have a daily routine. But I keep remembering what Bo In Lee told me after looking at the lines in my hand: "You need to begin your spiritual journey. Now."

At my doctor's insistence, I put the children into day-care three days a week. He also makes me promise to eat all my meals alone, in another room, while Bill tends the girls. I slowly begin to gain back the weight I have lost.

When the children are in day-care, I sporadically pick up

the mimeographed sheets Reverend Tanaka had given me and try to chant. It is very lonely. One voice vibrating in a hollow home.

When Fall comes, I sometimes walk down the leafy trail behind our cedar house and head toward the creek, carrying the mimeographed chants. I sit in a nest of brown crusty leaves and cross my legs. Gazing into the water rippling over moss covered rocks as it winds its way to nowhere, I open my mouth. "Na me ro sha cha mu," rolls out of me. I can feel my throat rumble. A lowing "N-a-h" emerges from before-it-was, pushing its way into creation, slowly disappearing. The sound drops into a still landscape, concentric circles of it lapping against the Fall leaves. Sound, borne on frost vapor. I draw in unsullied, silent new air. I pause. "M-a-y" slowly undulates its way up my chest, constricting in the tube of my throat, passing through my mouth, my ears the only witness of its birth. One voice crying out some primordial birth chant. Why am I chanting? Perhaps it is my cry of anguish. I have fallen in love with my children. I have not yet fallen in love with the demands of parenting.

～

Now, Winter has come.

I turn the yard-sale brown wood rocker toward the vast wall of window glass facing the woods. I pick up the white kitchen timer, twisting the dial to twenty minutes. Tick-tick-tick. A loud, annoying reminder bouncing against the white walls, cathedral ceiling, and bare wood floor.

Only twenty minutes. That's all I can stand of silence.

Tick. Tick. Tick. Tick. Tick. Tick. Tick. Tick.

I sit there tense, my stomach tight, trying to enter into

Buddhist mindfulness. A detached watching of thoughts passing. A spacious region where Buddhists apparently roam. *Why am I here?* For the same reason I arose at 5:30 on that morning in May. I seem to have lost my self. Perhaps I can find her here.

    Tick. Tick. Tick. Tick. Tick. Tick. Tick. Tick.

∽

Days pass.
Weeks pass.
Months pass.
Tick. Tick. Tick. Tick. Tick. Tick. Tick. Tick.

∽

Every afternoon, around two o'clock, I doggedly set the timer and sit in the rocker facing the woods. I silently intone a one-syllable mantra — *faith*. To quiet myself down. To try to drown out the ticking. I refuse to give up the timer. I commit myself to twenty minutes each day. No more. No less. Each minute evenly divided. I mentally compute. *Twelve hundred ticks.* The tick-tick-tick slowly builds, like jelly beans in a giant glass jar I am expected to count. I start to tense. *Is this the last tick?* Tick. *Is this one it?* Tick.

My stomach tightens in Pavlovian anticipation of the shrill shrieking alarm. Tick. On it goes. Tick. I give up any remaining hope of spiritual enlightenment. Of nirvana. Of holiness, sainthood, mystic transformation. BBRRIIIINNGG.

∽

I can't meditate, I decide, finally acknowledging failure. *I'll never be able to quiet myself. I'm going to give it up.* I settle into the rocking chair. I am coming to the end of every hope, dream, expectation I had for some spiritual experience. *Today will be the last day I do this,* I resolve. I feel sad. It didn't work. What I so desperately needed — whatever it was — I had not found. Not after months of trying. Not after almost a year. Spring will soon be here.

I turn the timer, sit in the chair, close my eyes. *Faith. Faith. Faith.* I hear the timer ticking in the background. Tick. Tick. Tick. My body slowly gentles. *Faith . . . faith . . . faith.*

Suddenly, time stops. My prayer bursts out of finite reality like a jet transcending the time barrier. Though my ears should be hearing the ticking of the timer, they hear nothing at all.

You have been waiting all these months for me to give up, I murmur in awe to this new indwelling silence. *It is humble inability you want, not my determination to succeed.*

I have shed time like a snake slipping from its skin. For one incredible moment, I am held in the embrace of pure silence.

noisy silence

*O*riginally, when Bill and I married, we had planned to remain childless, and our home reflected that. A modular-modern, cedar-sided rambler, the inside was more fireplace brick, wood floor, and glass window than wall. So when Kendra and Lisa joined us, they played in a modernistic home where the living room merged into the dining room which melted into the kitchen. In other words, we lived in an expensive one-room cabin. There were no silent places in our house.

I sometimes wondered if I would ever find that place of pure silence again. Or would my only memory of it be the exhausted sleep of a mother who felt brain-dead?

And what, exactly, was this silence that I was seeking? A walk-in-the-woods silence? A designing-a-computer-system silence? What was this yearning that drove me deeper and deeper into my quest? I didn't know, and sometimes it frightened me.

During all those days of sitting in silence punctuated by the raucous ticking of my timer, I at least had the comforting reassurance that time was passing in countable moments, that I couldn't be swallowed up into some vast emptiness. But on the day I stopped hearing the beat of the clock, silence opened a deeper portal into its mysteries. What lay ahead, I could not know. My main concern now was to continue to be a good mother and a good wife. This left me with a divided spirit. One part of me yearned to dwell in this new-found, silent world; the other anchored me securely to my love of children and husband. If I had to jettison one, it would have been my quest for silence.

To my surprise, however, I found a middle way.

~

"Let's play Legos," Kendra says to Lisa, dumping the contents of the cardboard box with a clatter onto the floor. It is 4:00 P.M. — fondly known among mothers as "arsenic hour." The productive work of shopping and cleaning are done for the day. Snack time is over; my children are wired for action. Somehow in the midst of these two bubbly "go-mobiles," I want a little silence before the evening shift of dinner, dishes, baths, and bedtime.

I plop myself down in the wood rocker, feeling its smooth, warm arms beneath me. The large, glass-walled living room has never been conducive to traditional furniture settings. Sofas and chairs end up scattered in unlikely locations. The rocker sits albatross-like in the middle of the living room.

"Let's build houses, Lisa," I hear Kendra's voice.

This will not work, I think to myself. I will never be able to quiet myself. Remembering the tick-tick-tick of the kitchen timer, I feel my body tensing as if ready for another battle with the sound barrier.

Many of my silent moments have occurred in this chair. Solid and safe, it rocks back and forth, back and forth, in a lulling movement. Today, the noise of my high-pitched children's voices scratches my worn nerves like barbed wire. Mothers have been known to lock themselves in the bathroom to gain a few moments of privacy.

I remember reading that Suzanna Wesley, the mother of John Wesley, founder of Methodism, often threw her floor-length skirt over her head to escape her numerous children. Whenever I try to retreat to another room for a few moments, however, Kendra and Lisa track me down. Before the door even closes, their voices raise with piteous pleas, questions, or cries. I give up. *If I am ever going to have a moment of silence, it's going to have to be right here,* I tell myself one day — *right next to my kids. And what safer place than with my children three feet away?*

But it seems a hopeless wish.

I begin to silently carry my one syllable word, *faith,* on my breath. *A boring word,* I think.

I squirm in the rocker. I can feel my children's noise hitting the barrier of my body and reverberating off it into space. *Faith. Faith. Faith.*

"Let's build a road."

"Okay."

"Let's make it yellow."

I hear another box of Legos being dumped with a crash onto the floor.

I begin to feel myself slipping down into silence. At the edge of one world, not quite in another. *It feels like that place just before you fall asleep,* I think. Their voices become muted. I feel as though an interior baby monitor turns on: mother's instinct will alert me if they need me. I am there — and I am not there.

It is as if I am sitting atop a gently sloping, sliding board of noise perched above an ocean of silence. I slip down its back. I glide down, the noise carrying me, into the watery, muted, imageless world of silence. My thoughts come slower and slower. The distraction of my children playing becomes the pathway into silence. *It's like the clock. The kitchen timer. Tick-tick-tick.*

I move into a very deep, still silence in which not even time dares intrude.

Strange, I think, *that noise should be the portal to silence. The gentle guard at the entryway.* The rocking stops. I am held motionless in silence.

"LISA, GIVE IT TO ME!" Kendra screams, grabbing a Lego out of her sister's hand.

My internal monitor goes off!

"Kendra," I hear my voice. Her name sounds sluggishly heavy on my tongue, like mud dredged from a silt-filled river. "You don't get things by yelling," I caution her. Lisa is clutching the red blocks in her chubby hand.

"LISA, PLEASE," Kendra wails.

Lisa remains the immutable sphinx, stubbornly placing her red blocks on her house.

"Look, Lisa," Kendra coaxes, holding up two handfuls of blocks. "I'll trade you all these green ones."

I watch Lisa weigh the trade.

"Okay," Lisa throws the red ones at Kendra and scoops up the green.

I close my eyes and gently rock. I have found a middle way.

Their back-and-forth chatter lulls me into stillness. I have made the discovery that my secret doorway to silence is noise.

unsettled

*I*nitially, silence was like a friendly neighbor who visited, upon invitation. I would invite quiet into my life. I prepared a place for it, my rocking chair, and a time. And into that tiny space, I would allow silence to squeeze.

It was a very ordinary silence, a time for peaceful reflection. It brought back memories of times when I would sit at my office desk thinking about a design problem. Like pondering a chess move, my attention would quietly sink into an inner mental world where I contentedly played with my thoughts.

That was silence, as I knew it, up to the time of the clock — when time itself disappeared.

Now, when I enter the silence, I am in a place I have never traveled to before, as child or adult. A world not inhabited by the mind but by some ancient primordial memory carried in my body. Thoughts — even dark anxious ones — bob above and around and through me, but I am like a ghost unable to hold onto or process them. It is as though I have come into a vast empty concert hall where a hauntingly beautiful melody is being played. As each note washes over me, I want to grab it, keep it forever, but it floats by.

I find myself in a strangely quiet place quite unlike any other I have known. Because it is unfamiliar, uncommon, I am not sure I want to stay. Is this silence safe? Healthy? Normal?

Like someone falling in love, I had assumed that I understood this companion, silence. But, except for that stark, fear-filled moment over the glacier, I had seen only what I wanted to see — an idyllic silence that was comfortable, relaxing, safe. A place to recover and rejuvenate. Now in this strange timelessness, I am seeing a side of silence that I find disquieting. Disquieting because I can't control it. It is like an unasked-for pregnancy.

I fell in love with silence; I made love in this still, timeless place; and now, something unalterable is changing within me. What, I do not yet know.

Silence continues to woo me, leaving behind the fragrance of its elusive presence. In the midst of two very busy, very noisy children, deep quiet unexpectedly descends upon me.

~

"Let's go outside," Kendra looks up from her coloring, bored.

Lisa, reluctant to give up the garish crayoned scribble she is creating, says, "NO."

"Let's COOK," Kendra ups the ante. The sandbox is more gooey orange mud than sand. "Cooking" requires swim suits and a hose-down to get back into the house.

"Okay," Lisa agrees, giving her picture one final blaze of color. Five minutes later, I hear the door being yanked open, and

Kendra hollering as they race toward the mud, "Let's make a pie."

The house is suddenly quiet. Silence beckons, like a lover waiting. My movements become slower and slower as silence wraps me in its embrace. So hungry am I for it, it feels as though I am being swept into a dense cloud.

I stop.

I move to the rocking chair and sit down.

Please don't overwhelm me, I ask it. *There's the cleaning. The laundry needs to be folded. I haven't started dinner.*

I sink into the silence, losing time.

Silence comes this way now. It embarrasses me. I no longer chant mantras or utter one-syllabled words to quiet myself. Like a woman impregnated with a seed, silence is growing inside me without my advice or urging.

I begin to know quiet in a way I have never known it before. No black hole of emptiness or infinite nothingness. Rather, a fullness, a coming-into, a vast unexplored region.

How can you be like this? I marvel. *How lovely. How beautiful,* I murmur before words become too heavy to think.

In this fullness, unexplored and inexplicable, I ponder: How did this silent guest who came for a temporary visit make herself so at home in my life, so indispensable? How did she become so important to me?

how did this happen?

*S*ilence,

I touch my body
above the womb, below the heart,
where you are growing.

How did this happen?
what love-making?
what lover?

I use birth control,
a proven method,
the notime method —
no time for surprises.

What night did I forget?

Your feet thrust against my former life.
Your light warms my rib cage.
Your fingers and toes pierce my life,
sightless and soundless.

How are you birthed?
What shall I name you?
Where shall I put you?

And can you at least tell me,

Are you pink?

or blue?

PART II: STRUGGLING WITH SILENCE

Why, since you wounded
this heart, don't you heal it?
And why, since you stole it from me,
do you leave it so,
and fail to carry off what you have stolen?

— "Spiritual Canticle," St. John of the Cross

SILENCE

sixth sense

I just want to be a wife and a mother, I say fretfully to the silence closing in on my life.

Silence has begun to overflow the boundaries of my prayer time. It is pressing out of the room in which I have tried to contain it, the portal I know as my quiet sitting time. Silence is enveloping me at unexpected moments: while I am vacuuming, when I am setting the table for dinner. I feel I am a pregnant woman whose water has broken. In its watery wake, I am enveloped in overwhelming joy — but it is a joy looking into the jaws of fear.

What labor lies ahead?

~

For over a year, I have enjoyed the intoxicating presence of silence. Since both the children are now in school for a few hours every day, I have the house, luxuriously quiet, to myself. I have reconciled myself to this new form of silence. More than the friendly companion I first knew, it is now a constant presence that makes love to something deeply hidden within me. I no longer fight it, as I did when the timer ticked its incessant beat two years ago.

Even though this silence is deeper, I have found it still has predictable limits, boundaries. Unexpectedly, it will roll over me like an incoming tide swamping the beaches of my life, but eventually it will recede to whatever strange sea of origin it came from. Then I am once again a mother checking her watch to make sure the kids are picked up on time, a wife listening to her husband recount his work day.

This silence is beautiful. More than I imagined, it is warm and luxurious, welcoming and kind. The only uncomfortable aspect is that I cannot control it. I cannot make it happen. I cannot measure how long it will last.

～

I gradually grow comfortable in the knowledge that this silence, though different from what I had expected, is safe. And I think to myself, *This is the end of the journey. I have met a wonderful companion in silence. I am profoundly grateful for my good fortune.* Naïve, I do not realize that silence might want more of me.

～

It is an early Spring day. The tips of some trees have begun to swell and redden, a sign that buds will soon erupt. The moist, brown-humus'd banks of the creek are erupting into green, as thousands of skunk cabbage shoots thrust their olive-greened spears out of the ground. In a few days, they will unfurl their leaves, carpeting the valley with emerald, fan-shaped brilliance.

I hold a mug of coffee and quietly gaze out the sliding glass doors of the dining room, watching the sun's rays filter through the forest onto the morning-dark earth. Except for a solitary bird's cry heralding a new day, all is still. I slip without effort into my world of silence, the quiet of my stilled self sinking into the gentle wooded day.

~

That is my last memory.
Before the change.

~

Time begins again. The pacing of it, the movement of the clock hand over the face in the kitchen. I look down. I am still holding my coffee mug, the coffee still warm. Has a nanosecond passed? Or an hour? My body's sense of time has skipped a beat. I feel frightened, terrified really. Something irreversible has changed inside me: Silence has stepped across a new boundary.

~

It is hard to explain this part of the story. Hard, not because of the experience itself — though that was frightening enough — but because, like describing a perfume, I can only describe the effect of the fragrance.

Perhaps an analogy will help. People who have had near-death experiences explain the transforming moment this way: They have not volunteered for the experience, yet they have found themselves in some other topography that has nothing to do with the reality of their ordinary human life. It terrifies them; it angers them. They are left between two worlds — some cosmic space and some finite reality — and they don't know how to relate. How to live. How to explain.

Mystics, too, have a similar experience. They are praying, saying they want to be closer to the Divine. Really meaning it, earnestly wanting it. Then some cosmic trap door opens, and they find themselves free-falling into some reality that is more real than their own flesh, but has no connection to their lived experience. They walk around in a daze for days, weeks, months, hardly able to function in reality.

To understand the enormous difficulty of my transition, I can only describe how I felt immediately afterward: Whereas before, my reality was derived from taste, touch, smell, sound, sight, now I had a sixth sense.

One moment I was quietly standing beside my sliding glass doors enjoying the intoxicating beauty of Spring, serenely surrendering to its silence — and BAM — the next moment, my former five-sense "mental operating system" was obsolete. Some new version had been installed. And I had no operator's manual. The billions of sense-based pieces of data immediately began to flow through this new structured reality.

I was more than a little upset. I was terrified.

I decided not to talk about it.

~

In the days, weeks, and months that followed, I felt as though my life were being washed away by a hurricane. The life I had lived, the way I had functioned, the routine I had created became the mindless debris of dislocated sensations.

I would find myself studying one page of a book while time ticked on, unable to make any sense of the words. When Bill would turn on the evening television, the fast rush of actors' emotions would hurtle themselves at me, overwhelming me, and I would flee the room.

Rather than the peaceful silence I had known, where thoughts bobbed around me like ducks, all the moorings were now gone. Like a person fighting a tidal wave, I was trying to hold onto my old ways when they had been swept away.

For the first time, I understood the Exodus. My heart cried out to those ancient Jews who, once they had crossed the Red Sea, wished they had died in Egypt.

I, too, wanted to go back — back to the comfortable silence that had enriched my life. I had trustingly followed this silence, and it had taken me away from my known world. Now, some strange waters rushed over me, sealing off my return forever.

This silence terrified me.

betrayed

I am now wed to you,
betrothed in secret wedding
not even asked but *stolen*,
unbeknownst to my own family
even to my own self.

You wooed the virgin hidden in me
bribing your way past my own senses.
You courted my spirit
hiding beneath my checkered past.
You bound it to you in holy matrimony
without even inviting *me*.

no human witness
I am unsure if divine.

I am left alone in my bed chamber
on this silk-sheeted bed.
You have wooed, wed, and gone
— the chamber windows open —
the curtain ruffling in your wake.

The sun is shining its morning welcome.
Am I to get out of bed?
What am I to do
now that I am no longer who I was
and cannot go back?

Shall I arise and go forth
into this same world
. . . differently?

I tremble, not knowing
— is there any other way?

the basement

I hear the basement door open. "Anybody down there?" my husband yells. I can't answer. I am too deep into prayer. From experience, I know my voice will not come back that quickly.

"Click." I hear the light switch go off. The door slams shut. Suddenly I am in impenetrable darkness.

I have been slowly re-connecting the dots within my life, reconstructing bits and pieces along a different reality. I now live concurrently in three different — and often conflicting — worlds. First, there is my life as wife and mother. Profoundly grateful for the monotony of everyday life, I cling to routine like a lost hiker following a compass setting. Then there is the time I spend in silence, a silence that continues to feel chaotic and unclear as I struggle to sort through the confusion of what has happened to me.

My third world, lying deep beneath my world as wife and mother, deeper than the swirling confusion of thoughts, is an inner core where I feel an unshakable confidence that all is well. Although the skin of my body literally crawls with anxiety, this center of my soul feels at peace — a peace that makes previous definitions pale in comparison.

Whereas before, peace had been a happy feeling, a contentment when things go my way, now peace requires nothing — not good fortune, good luck, or happy circumstances. It exists in and of itself, giving assurance like an emitting radar signal tuned into my quivering life.

I begin to suspect that a great gift is being given me — that I will one day see my self as God created me.

I am walking on the soil of my own soul.

~

I shiver and draw the time-softened afghan over me. It has been a hard weekend. Grandpa's birthday, a trip to the lake, swimming, cranky kids on the way home, sunburn.

The old, brown vinyl office chair I am sitting in creaks precariously backward. I am not ready to leave this basement and go upstairs. I sink back into troubled prayer, its signposts now familiar: The rushing thoughts. The sheer density of them. The heaviness of them. Gradually I am learning to stay very still in these troubled waters, watching my thoughts rush by. Less and less do they snag me, jerking me out of prayer. Basements, I have discovered, have little kinship with the human idea of peaceful silence. They have no need for centering prayer. They do not breathe in and out to slow themselves to quiet mindfulness. They are simply a vast, carved-out essence of silence.

Sometimes such silence is dense. Pitch-black basement silence is like that. It settles on you like a raven on a moonless night.

You open your eyes wide open, and it is as though you have no eyes at all. It is an impenetrable kind of silence.

~

I should be able to do this, I tell myself, standing up in the darkness.

The staircase should be on my right. I begin to grope my way through the cavernous basement, colliding with a two-drawer filing cabinet.

Where was that? I try to remember exactly where we had stowed the file in the junk-strewn basement.

I think I need to go a little more to the right. I take two steps sideways.

Okay, I think, *now I should be able to go straight forward.*

I run into a pole. I continue to grope, colliding with objects, feeling them, trying another course correction. Several minutes pass by. My frustration mounts. *I don't like you very much right now,* I chide silence. In prayer, I collide with mental objects; now, I'm colliding with physical.

I begin to feel the air gingerly with my hands, touching objects, repositioning myself, touching again, adding each object to my internal map, touching, mapping, touching, adjusting my new geography. Gradually my map expands and grows.

My hands reach out. My fingertips brush the wood of a door frame. I inch forward until I can firmly grasp the knob and turn it. I am now out of the storage area. Three strides ahead lies the first step of the basement stairwell.

Not bothering to turn on the light, I walk up, my feet remembering the steps to the first turn. At last I see a warm yellow light slicing its way beneath the bottom of the basement door.

I turn the knob. *Perhaps one day I'll navigate interior, unmapped silence the same way I learned to feel my way through this basement. Then, perhaps, my three worlds will be reunited.*

But for now, I am grateful to leave. I open the door, and give a last glance downstairs. My eyes are already unable to adjust to the pitch-black darkness I have just left behind.

I shut the door. In the basement, I can fall frighteningly deep into my soul. Up here, I am in charge.

the mall

At exactly 4:00 P.M. on Wednesday, I pull into my favorite parking space at the Columbia Mall. I like this spot for three reasons. First, other shoppers don't. Second, it sits on the exit ramp. Third, I can take one last look at wildly untamed trees, unrepentant grass, and the blue water from Kittamakundi Lake in front of me — and promise myself I am more than what I buy.

I sit here for a moment, mentally girding myself for the shop-'til-you-drop dream. I put the car keys in my pocket, open the car door, and head toward the modern mausoleum of material merchandise. I open the glass door — and step into the antiphonal world of silence.

~

This mall has two levels. Twenty years ago, it was the largest one in Maryland. Now it is average, having long lost its square-footage fame to mega-malls elsewhere. Inside a fountain spouts water into a receiving pool, which is periodically re-invented to serve as a holding tank for styrofoam snow at Christmas and potted plants at Easter. It also serves as a runway for models. But today it is a fountain with copper coins glimmering against its pool-blue lining.

I walk to the second floor rail overlooking the fountain. I need to get my bearings. Below, a mother is helping her son toss a coin. Two women stroll by pushing baby carriages, chatting to each other. A single woman in a tailored beige suit walks by carrying a drink-filled cup, her staccato heels echoing across the floor.

I am faced with my first decision. Where to go? I need a birthday gift, and new underwear. I could go left. There is a department store at that end. I could go right. There is a department store at that end. I could walk past the jewelry store, shoe store, book store, and clothing store on the left. I could walk down past the shoe, book, clothing, jewelry stores on the right. My other option is to take the escalator down and do the same, or eat Mexican, Chinese, Greek, or deli. Or I could wait and eat Mexican, Chinese, or Italian at the other end of the mall.

I have entered the silence of sameness.

～

My eyes begin to glaze over as I walk down the left side of the second level. Each person I see carries one of five things — a child, food, a plastic or paper bag, a boyfriend, or a girlfriend. I will soon join the plastic/paper-bag crowd. I am going to a department store sale.

I hear snatches of conversation.

"I think the dress at Gantos looks best on you."

"Meredith, we'll get you ice cream *after* Mommy goes to Victoria's."

"Hey, get a look at those girls."

"John, I need to stop at the card shop before we leave. Remind me!"

I keep walking. Past The Gap, The Limited, Lerners, Casual Corner. Past FootLocker and Naturalizer. I am wondering if I really, *absolutely* have to have new underwear. Can what I have, tattered though it is, last another year?

No, Barbara, this is the last day of the semi-annual lingerie sale, I mentally chide myself. *Think of all the money you will save.*

~

We think we elude silence if we go to a mall. It is filled with bustling, bright-eyed, chattering people. But silence is there. Not the living silence of a beach at dawn, but the glassy-eyed silence of a mannequin.

Silent images stalk me and my pocketbook. *I could use a new dress, new jeans, new coat. Oh! Look at those gargoyles — and they're on sale,* I hear myself silently saying.

Mall silence is like King Tut's tomb — refurbished twenty-first century style, missing only the embalmed body.

Sometimes I go to the mall because I'm bored. Or I go because the sagging body I saw in the mirror that morning needs a new dress. I get lost in the dream of if-I-just-had-some-more-money. The mall is like a television screen without the glass. I can walk right onto the set.

Sometimes — and this is the most ironic of all — I go to the mall to try to buy something that will create an image of silence in my own home — a still-life painting, a Shaker-type piece of furniture, a new wood cutting board for the kitchen. I sometimes prefer the illusion of silence — the happy, pocketbook-toting, mall-mannequin version of it — to the silence of my own soul.

Once in a while I wonder what I am doing here — but it's too late. Alice-in-Wonderland has fallen, once again, into the dark hole.

the hotel

*T*he narrow hallway is dimly lit, the wall-mounted light fixtures vying with the dull glow of the EXIT signs. The carpet is thread-bare and worn with dark stains on its faded, wine-red oriental splendor.

I am once again in a hotel, its silence beginning to invade my tired, vulnerable body.

I remember how excited I was, years ago, when I took my first trip to California as an information systems specialist. The hotel with the artificial-ivy-draped balconies was paradise; the fillet mignon superb. I used the swimming pool, the exercise room, the jacuzzi. I watched TV till midnight. Even car rental was thrilling.

Now, twenty years and dozens of hotels later, I no longer have the same enthusiasm when I accept occasional freelance consulting jobs or travel for writing.

I turn the key in the lock. This is the moment when I *hope* that hotel silence will surprise me.

Unlikely, I say to myself. *This is an econo room in Missoula.*

The door gives way. A heavy musky odor, the memory of cigarette smoke trapped in mildew, pours into the hallway. I courageously swing the door open.

~

The brown motif of the room overwhelms me like muddy water from a swollen river: a brown-flowered, thin bedspread slightly alleviating the solid brown color of the carpet that is the identical shade of the brown upholstered chair, which accents the non-matching pair of brown formica night stands and offsets the beige ceramic table lamps, which illuminate the solid brown veneer headboard over which is hung a brown landscape with brown trees, brown sky, brown barn, brown flowers, brown fence, brown trash barrel, signed in brown by an artist named "Anixes Orpinas."

The silence sinks over me like the recent death of a loved one. It presses me deeper into the brown carpet.

~

With practiced skill, I roll my suitcase to the corner of the room, lay it flat, and hang up the few things that need a wrinkle-free environment. I check the bathroom for towels and soap. They are always there.

It is 5:00 P.M. Too early for dinner. Six long hours lie ahead, stacked atop each other in sinking heavy flatness.

My early-career infatuation with hotel rooms ended when, on my third trip, I realized that rented-room decor was mass-produced monotony manufactured in muted color tones. While I analyze the latest trends with perennial hopefulness that some mystic will become a hotel decorator, it has not yet happened. I have yet to make friends with hotel silence. And now, I am its captive till check-out. Of necessity, I engage in a tentative, short-lived, mutually disagreeable relationship with it.

I sit in the only upholstered chair. Its back cuts into my shoulder blades. I get up and plump the pillows on the bed. They are too few. The top of the headboard cuts into my upper spine. I finally pull a book out of my suitcase and lie on my stomach, arching my back into an ache as I rest my chin on the two mushy pillows.

An hour passes.

The unnatural silence reverberates as doors down the corridor open and slam shut — other people entering their identically decored cubicles of silence.

I am afraid the silence will suffocate me during the night when my guard is down. It will take its cigarette-musky breath and creep into my spirit and smother it.

I don't believe this room wants guests. It has a sullen, solitary nature that displays the worst side of itself immediately when a human being enters. I check to make sure the Gideon Bible is present. I pick up the cable television guide. Sometimes I can hurtle the silence out with the loud, animated voices of TV. Tonight, my choices are slim: "The Fugitive," "Dennis the Menace," "Luscious Night." I decide to co-exist with the silence.

I pick up my book and head for the bathroom. Maybe a bath will help.

~

I turn on the spigot, blasting water into the enamel tub, burying the iron-water brown stain beneath a hot waterfall. I slip off my clothes and step in, trying to avoid the grimy white rubber flowers adhered to its bottom. I take my water-hot washcloth and paste it against the back of the tub before I lean into its cold metallic embrace, shiver, and slowly sink down.

Neck-deep in warm water is the only safe place I can find in the deadening silence of hotel rooms. Even in mahogany wood Queen Anne business suites with personal refrigerators and coffee makers, I still retreat to the tub.

In this warm silence of lapping water, the brown painting over the brown bed resting on the brown carpet recedes from my mind.

Silence — the one I now carry within me — has a complex personality unlike the simple silence I once knew. It is querulous when I attempt to dictate how it *should* be present in my life. But when I surrender, admitting defeat, I find this silence willing to teach me its secrets. Recognizing my discouragement tonight, it tentatively peeks out from its warm water cocoon, a lithesome Nile creature who uninhibitedly dances from the tomb. I lie in the luxurious splendor of it, the book forgotten until the tepid water arouses me from my dreamily still world.

I dry off, hoping this silence will emerge with me from the bathroom to face the deadly silence of the brown decor. I open the door. The unrepentantly silent brown furniture flattens any friendly overtures. These two silences are not sisters.

~

Hotel silence is the loneliest silence I know.

lost

*J*ust over the hill, Barbara, there's a wonderful view of the valley," Bill says, pointing toward the faint trail through dense mountain blueberry bushes.

"It looks like an animal trail, Bill," I answer, fearing it would peter out.

"No, it goes right to the top. You won't have any problem."

"Kendra," I call to my now six-year-old daughter, "come with me." She takes my hand. I pour my meager harvest of black-skinned berries into Bill's hand. Kendra and I leave Bill and Lisa sitting on a large rock.

"Don't squash them," I hear Bill tell her. Mentally I can see her squishing the tough-skinned blueberries between her stubby fingers and licking the juice off them. She is not a neat, tidy child.

Botanists claim that Dolly Sods, an untamed wilderness area in West Virginia, has a climate as harsh as the Canadian tundra. Though only early September, the late afternoon air is already crisp and the wind brisk. Overhead the sun casts an ending Summer brilliance onto the mountain, making every color intense.

"Go toward the tree," Bill had suggested.

"What tree?" I had asked, peering toward the barren ridge.

"You'll see it when you get up the trail a bit further," he had promised.

"Daddy said to head for the tree, Kendra," I explain, watching the wind whip her black hair into playful swirls as we climb. Now we stand on a gray, silver-flecked boulder looking across a vast plateau. Here and there, we see tiny scrub pine trees. They look like bonsai orphans that somehow have gotten separated from their Japanese pots. Trimmed into grotesque shapes by the unrelenting wind, snow, and ice, they lead a dwarf-like existence here, sinking their roots around and under the dry stony earth.

"Maybe that's it," I suggest, pointing to a tree whose only virtue is that it is dead and therefore somehow distinctive.

We head toward the tree that seems to mock the harsh natural forces with its upraised, sun-grayed limbs.

"See if you can hop this far, Kendra," I say leaping from one sun-warmed rock to the next. "Whoever touches the ground loses," I yell, hopping to the next. Kendra goes airborne.

We forget about the trail, intent on not touching the ground.

Five minutes later, we stand beside the dead tree. *Where is the panoramic view Bill promised us,* I wonder to myself gazing out on a vast barren field filled with boulders.

In the distance, I can see a slight rise. *Maybe that was the ridge we were supposed to hike toward,* I think to myself. Everywhere I look, there are trees and false ridges — the word hikers use when they wearily crest a mountain top only to find it is a knob against the landscape of a higher peak. We are standing in a slight depression.

The wind picks up, sweeping across the rocks, cooling off their hard-won afternoon warmth. The gray rocks are growing darker by the second as the sun sinks deeper into the sky. Soon they will be hidden beneath a solid blanket of darkness.

Where is the trail, I ask myself, turning around expecting to see its traces between the rocks. I see nothing.

Maybe if we are quiet enough, I can hear their voices. "Kendra, let's listen and see if we can hear Daddy and Lisa."

We stand in silence, the wind whipping over us, swirling our hair into our faces.

Nothing.

I strain to hear any sign of life — a voice, the sound of a car. A minute passes. The shadows are quickly growing longer and longer, the rocks darker. In perhaps an hour, it will be dusk in the Sods, and the temperature will start dropping rapidly.

We're lost, I think silently. *And I have my child with me.* I am terrified.

"Kendra, I think we've lost the trail. We're going to have to start looking for it."

I grab her hand and half drag her off the rock by the tree. We begin making our way across the boulders, unsure if we are getting closer — or farther away. It's not a game any more.

~

The silence of untamed wilderness holds special terror for me. When Bill and I had hung, motionless, in a tiny funicular over the vast glacier between Mt. Blanc and Italy, I had felt that terror. Now, with night descending on this rocky ridge, I feel it again.

"I'm going to call Daddy, Kendra. If he answers, I'll know

which way to find the trail."

"B-I-L-L-L!" I hurtle the word into the darkening sky. The wind swoops down, catching it in a gaping vortex, and to my horror, swallows it.

The wind speaks no language I know. It owns this land. We are the intruders. We have become part of it — not knowing, not understanding, just a windswept particle of life buffeted by the wind moving like a relentless wave across the barren landscape.

Terrified, I force myself to listen. Our safety now rests in understanding, and not fleeing from, this silence.

The inner world of quiet I descend into no longer terrifies me. This sixth sense has become part of my life, not the bottomless pit I once feared. No matter how intense my outer turmoil, inwardly I land on the solid soil of my soul. I am learning to listen to it — and trust it — as a guide.

Now I know it is the only path that might get us back to safety.

～

Slowly I turn, feeling the wind hit my face. *The wind . . .* I stand there, letting its silent force swirl into my own silence. Waiting. Waiting. It is hitting my left cheek. Suddenly I remember: *The wind was on my left cheek when we climbed up the trail. I need to turn until it is on my right cheek.*

You are my compass, I tell the wind.

"Kendra," I tug her tired body after me, "we need to go this way." I look down at her. She is strangely subdued. She senses my fear and it scares her. *Oh God, help us,* I silently beg.

We stumble over rocks, no longer the warm, silver-flecked

friends I remembered but now cold, sinister strangers indifferent to our fate. It gets darker and darker.

We crest a tiny hill. In the depression below, I see a gravel road. "Kendra," I shout, "That's the ROAD! Our car's down there. We're safe."

I quickly reposition myself. *If the road is there, the trail ought to be . . .*

"There it is, Kendra. The trail."

"Barbara? Kendra?" I hear Bill calling.

"We're here," I yodel back.

Minutes later, I am in his arms, safe.

As we climb down the hill, the wind begins to recede. I feel a tingle of awe and amazement rising inside me. *Here, beneath the summit, the wind doesn't blow. The thickets of berry bushes protect us,* I realize. *Had I gotten lost in the scrubby undergrowth, the compass-like direction of the wind would have been caught, like a fish in a net, on the branches. We would have remained lost.*

My inner silence found for me the only safe route home — a quiet listening to the forces of nature I feared most. Instead of fleeing from the impenetrable silence of the wind, I stayed rooted within the vortex of it. I found another way.

I entrusted the safety of myself and my child, for the first time, to the silence within me.

new orleans

*I*t is 1992. I am alone in a yet another hotel room, this time in New Orleans. Bill has left for a meeting. I haven't sat in silence for days. Getting the children to their aunt's house, packing, catching the plane, touring the French Quarter have exhausted me. *Now,* I think to myself, *I can relax.*

Almost eight years have passed since I first experienced what I call my "sixth sense" of silence. I find that I can no longer function at the mega-speed I had once considered normal. Before, I would be time-sharing two tasks and planning three more at the same time. I knew exactly how long it took to drive to school, piano lessons, ballet, pom poms, the grocery store, and post office. I could estimate within a minute or two how long I'd be in each location. My day looked like a master sergeant's drill dream of precision. Sometimes at the end of the day, I'd mentally recount the things I had accomplished. Twenty tasks within four hours was not uncommon.

I can still do that now — if an emergency requires it — but

it would be a mega-warp speed totally contrary to my current pace. Time, I have found, has little to do with the astronomically correct clock in Greenwich, England, by which we set our watches. Time, in silence, is simply space. It has no chronology.

The high-tech world counts time by meetings and deadlines; the farmer by dawn and dusk. I now time my world by space. The space between tasks is as valued as the task itself.

My family, especially my husband, recognized this even sooner than I. "You seem far away," Bill said one day as I folded laundry. Bill could see something was changing. What, he did not know, and I did not know how to tell him.

It seemed as though silence had thrown a beacon of light onto the dark soil of my soul, a place long untilled, lying fertile beneath societal expectations. The more I walked upon my own soul, the more I realized that my life, as I was living it, was artificial turf. The roots of that turf — the need to please — reached all the way back to my childhood.

~

As a little girl, I had been somewhat solitary. I usually had only one friend — not because I was shy, but because I didn't want to be bothered with any more. During the Summer, I read, I walked, I sat on the screen porch daydreaming and watching birds. My memories are more of trees and rocks and grass than people. As the years went by, I forgot all the memorable events the rest of my family remembered.

As I grew older, I became acutely aware that my behavior, my desires, did not match those of my classmates. When puberty came, I was enamored with boys — but not enough to wear make-up, flirt, or talk endlessly about them at slumber parties as the other girls did. Frightened of being left behind, however, I chose their goals of marriage, children, and career rather than find my own.

I dated one man — and married him. A good, kind, wonderful man. I had a career. I adopted my children. I "did" normal things, but none of them made me feel normal.

As I added the interlocking pieces of wife, career, children, church, and volunteer to my facade of "belonging," I only felt more confused. It was into this context that silence had entered my world through the temporary breech of my husband's near death. Once it lodged in my body, however, I couldn't bear to part with it. Instinctively, I knew that silence led the way home, back to the solitary child I had abandoned long ago.

~

Bill closes the door to our hotel room, and I sit down in the nearest chair, eager to re-unite with the silence that has become my ballast and strength. It seems my life is more real in silence than it is in my role as wife and mother. While such thoughts frighten me, I reassure myself, *This is a passing phase.* Yet I wonder, *Is it?*

As I fall into silence, it is as though I am entering into the familiar descent, one I have gone through numerous times before to this silent world. Only this time, I am talked to. Out of silence I hear one word as though it were written on my heart.

"Now."

The same word that had been spoken to me at that Summer camp years ago, when Bo In Lee gazed at my hand and said, "You must begin your spiritual journey. *Now.*" But this time, the "now" is different. In one trembling instant, my facade — the one painstakingly built according to societal architecture — is flattened to rubble.

The signs have been there for some time. About a year ago, I had begun to have trouble breathing. Sometimes my throat would constrict to the size of a straw, and I would suck air in with a terrifying wheezing sound, frantic I was about to die. Though on inhalers, I failed to match the profile of an asthmatic. My attacks were rapid. Violent. Overwhelming. It was as though I suffered some strange malady — a chronic-fatigue syndrome of the spirit.

Why? I asked, my eyes welling with tears. *What is wrong with me? What should I do?*

The answer, gentle and still, is unshakably certain: *Be who you are created to be.*

~

Astonishment begins to wash through me. I remember the little girl. The silent walks. The daydreams. The not-quite-needing friends. The joy of just being. Lost in thought. Wondering. The continual desire to fit into a structure — the knowing I did not.

I began to understand why my life felt so disjointed. Groomed from birth through death to participate, I was expected to go to birthday parties, school, clubs, and church, and build my own community by marriage and children.

My natural bent toward solitude was a constant irritant against this societal expectation. I was not taught how to integrate my need for aloneness into the needs of community. Though solitude enthralled me as a child, it was so ill-received the few times

I let it peek out, I came to see it as taboo. Gradually, I learned to hide this desire, as though it were a deformity or malfunction.

I had buried my silence-seeking self.

Whenever I felt anxious or uncomfortable, instead of stilling myself in solitude, I would immerse myself in new activities. I drove silence from my mind.

~

Tears gush out, pouring down my cheeks.

"Now."

The word begins to echo like a mantra in my mind, a faint beat of hope. It is time to go back to my roots. To bring my love of solitude out of hiding.

anger

*T*hat's mine," she screams, her face contorted in black rage. Her sister is wearing one of her blouses without permission. We are standing in a parking lot.

"Get in the car," I snap curtly, too tired to negotiate yet another argument between them.

She utters another volley of abuse, "Give it back to me, you JERK."

"Kendra, be quiet," I say, my voice tight and thin with tension. "Put your seat belt on. If you say one more word, I'm taking you home."

Without even looking at her, I can mentally see her black eyes narrowing to slits as she slams her body down into the passenger seat, fastens her belt, and glares down at the book she has brought. I ease the car out of the parking lot. For the next thirty minutes, I will be with an angry teen-age daughter.

~

It's been two years now since Bill and I decided to separate. After twenty-four years of marriage, I put my suitcase in my car and drove to a near-by apartment. The reasons were complex, but one thing I do know: it was the most painful day of my life.

~

Today I have agreed to drive Kendra to the shop where the transmission on her car has been repaired. Out of the corner of my eye, I can see her long, dark hair spilling over her shoulders. Her trademark John-Lennon, round-rimmed, dark sunglasses. Her gray sweats and rubber-and-nylon sandals. Her thrust-out, sultry lower lip. She is no longer the child I adopted thirteen years ago when she was four.

We wait for the light to change. I watch the cars stream by. Rush hour is building. In the silence of the car, I hear sniffles. *It must be her allergies again,* I think. Then I see her hand reach furtively up to her cheek. She is crying.

Tears of frustration in subterranean spaces I know nothing of. No words from me right now will help.

We hit a straight stretch of three-lane highway. I increase my speed to sixty-five. Silence slowly settles in over us. Her sniffling stops. The morning sun glares through the window, and I flip my visor down. Soon we join the ant-like procession of cars heading north on the parkway.

Is it being adopted? An early trauma in Korea? My divorce? The stress of being a teen? All of the above? Probably, I decide, remembering my own teen-age years. I remember screaming at my father. Running out of the house, hysterical. *What was it about? I can't even remember.*

Silence has become the only safe language between us.

I turn onto the exit ramp heading toward the transmission repair shop. It will be a long drive down this road filled with detours and traffic lights.

The silence settles in even deeper over us. She is reading. She has tuned me out of her life. Her body — one that cameramen photograph for ad agencies — has a natural litheness to it, an exotic elegance. Not looking at her, I know her hair sparkles with burgundy highlights. Her slender body has a ballet-like regalness to it. In a photographer's hand, she becomes limpid and responsive — like clay to be molded into alluring shapes. Now she is modeling rage and anger as perfectly, as beautifully, as is humanly possible. Rather than hating the moment and all the recent months that have brought us to this, I find myself in awe.

I don't know how to love her right now, I admit. *What is a mother's love?* I ask myself. *Maybe it is accepting that she needs something I cannot give.*

We are nearing the shop, but I know I won't recognize it. Finally I speak. "I may need your help to spot this place."

Silence. No sign that I have been heard. I feel a slight flutter of anger. *Oh well,* I think, *I'll just have to find it on my own.*

We pass a muffler shop and bear down on a traffic light. With one elegant gesture — as penetrating as Michelangelo's God-touching-man in the Sistine Chapel, my daughter points. One red-tipped finger. I gaze in that direction. There on the corner is the shop, Jake's Auto Transmission. I ease into the left lane and flip on the turn signal. We are almost there.

Old cars line the lot, neatly queued in parking spaces, headlights uniformly aimed out. I pull up to her battered '88 station wagon and stop. "Why don't you check to see if you can get it started while I go inside."

Without a word, she steps out and slams the car door. I pull around the corner, park, and go inside. "I need to pay," I tell the attendant. Five minutes later, I push open the shop door to go out and walk around the corner to say good-bye.

Where is the car? I wonder, scanning the row of vehicles.

There is one empty space.

Then I know. My daughter is gone. *She got in and took off!*

All that is left is the exhaust of her silent rage.

I walk slowly toward my car. Strangely, I have come to peace with the silence that has fallen between my daughter and myself.

Sometimes, there are just times to be silent.

PART III: BUILDING SILENCE INTO A LIFESTYLE

She lived in solitude,
in solitude she made her nest
and all alone her lover
led her in solitude,
wounded in solitude by love.

— "Spiritual Canticle," St. John of the Cross

alone

I live alone now.

Perhaps not forever, but for now.
Gone the 19-year-old who married
tossing hamburgers onto second-hand china
while studying Chinese history.
Perhaps it was the real thing,
perhaps not.

But it is in the silence
that the final reckoning must come.

We have become a different sort of family
stretched 22.5 miles in length
odometered across acres of buried hope.

A wintered respite weathered in silence.

I live alone now.

the redwoods

I quickly glance at the National Park Service guidebook lying on the passenger seat. *That looks like the turn-off,* I decide, veering off the California highway onto a windy road. It is 6:00 A.M. I have hastily thrown my boots, water bottle, and an orange into a backpack, leaving my friend Anita asleep in the motel. *How could she get sick?* I wonder, knowing of her intense desire to see the redwood forest during our month-long vacation.

"They're one of the oldest living things in the world, Barbara," she had exclaimed, with excitement dancing in her blue eyes. Now her eyes are watering as she fights a feverish cold.

Years ago, Bill and I had visited a California redwood forest — a national park teaming with snapshot-shooting tourists capturing the moment forever of people posing in hollowed-out sequoias. I had read the plaques honoring this hall-of-fame grove. It was hard, I had decided then, to relate to a tree.

Now, I am back in redwood country. It is my first vacation since Bill and I have separated. I am slowly reconstructing my life, visiting the children daily, writing, working. But mostly, I am alone. Sometimes the loss is so sharp, it is bearable only if I breathe slowly. I hold the pain of it in the middle of my silence hoping, like labor, it will pass from pain to new life.

I have also experienced joy. The joy of discovering I am "me" simply because I prefer peas to carrots for dinner. Or that I often need to sit silent in my rocking chair gazing at some unseeable inner space.

I hope one day that these two irreconcilable opposites — pain and joy — will be reconciled. Now, at my friend Anita's urging, I am traveling to the sequoia forest. Alone.

~

I begin an upward ascent, my Ford Escort easily swinging into each hairpin turn on this cool, sunny morning. The black-top road soon gives way to hard-packed dirt. A seven-year drought has dried it into a parched dust that billows out from beneath my spinning wheels.

After several minutes of ascent through fields and farms, I begin to worry.

Where are the redwoods? Maybe this is the wrong road. There is no sign of giant trees. I swing around another corner. And another.

I give the steering wheel one hard twist to the left, spinning around a corkscrew curve, and . . .

My God!

Just like that. I have landed — a Lilliputian in the land of giants.

~

I careen the car to a halt in the center of the road and stare in stunned silence. A vast, timeless world sinks over me, crushing me in its length and breadth and depth, my comprehension of it diminishing to the size of a single second caught in a canyoned eternity. I am awed — and overwhelmed.

Behind me lies the ordinary road I drove on, a full-sized, two-lane road. Before me, it has shrunk to a human-traced line of dirt beneath the three-hundred-foot-tall towering giants dusting off their feet in the early morning dawn.

Behind me, the roadside vegetation serves a purpose. It marks the boundary between plowed field and bulldozed road. Before me, it is no more than an unswept floor.

Behind, I am an important creation — a human being — the direct descendant of Eve. Before these century-old giants, my superiority seems irrelevant, like having a high IQ when you're hungry.

For several seconds, I stand in stunned silence, unable to comprehend my diminishment.

~

I gently reach out to touch one of the giants, its matted, felt-like bark strange beneath my finger tips. I feel I've come home. After the confusion of the past two years trying to understand my need for solitude, I am like a child reaching with relief into her mother's arms.

Here, I feel a kinship. Forgotten giants in a world of sky

scrapers and rockets. Bound to the forest, mute, these trees can only give their wisdom to the ones who come to them. Standing beneath their aging limbs, I find comfort — as though I, too, could be rooted in such silence.

Tearing myself away, I return to my car and slowly continue down the road, drawn deeper into this quiet-magic world.

After fifteen minutes, I turn the car into a tiny parking area scooped out of the forest floor. Ahead lies a trail.

I lock the car, hearing the click echo through the forest, and cross the road. Silently, I step onto the fibrous path.

~

It's like a cavernous world, I think gazing up at the green-tufted giants. My footsteps sink into a century of fallen brown bark-hair shed by the slivering sides of sequoias. The sound of my boots disappears into the muffled world as I creep through the forest. A step. A pause. One of the giants has fallen, years, decades, perhaps centuries ago. I climb on top of it and sit, unable to contain the joy that silently soars up into the dark-needle'd canopy of green-firred limbs.

The sun splays golden shafts of light through the forest, the gauzy glimmer of them bathing the forest floor in an iridescent glow.

No one other than myself has yet ventured into the early morning musing of these trees.

I can almost feel them stretching upward with a yawn, as though unbending from a century of shadowed night. With their feet cool in the dusky shadow-world beneath their own boughs, they do slow calisthenics toward the heavens above, sending the sun's warmth down through their capillary veins to the forest feet below.

I lie on my back, stretched out on the bark, idly gazing upward.

Overhead, the trees play an early morning match with the rising sun, batting its rays back with green-needled racquets. Few escape its greeny boughs. Dust motes dance in a solar mist of angled sunshine.

I sink into a peaceful silence, wrapped, a timeless orphan, in the embrace of centuries. The trees close ranks around me as I free fall out of my human time into theirs.

No sound disturbs my reverie.

No jet streaks across the sky in early morning roar.

No squirrel scrambles across a crust-dry layer of leaves.

No bird sings through the forest.

I am utterly alone.

In the silence of sequoias.

Such a strong silence. It steps effortlessly through my fears. I marvel. I feel my body quieting within me, sinking into the forest's movement — a time that is moving slower, and s l o w e r. Until my time is so slow, I know — for one shimmering timeless moment — all will always be well.

the house

$\mathcal{I}$ bought my house, I think, because of the wood floors. The day before I signed the contract, I sat on the floor, alone, in the empty house. I needed to know what kind of silence I was going to live in within the cream-colored plaster walls.

Morning sun streamed through the front window making its slow passage across the newly varnished hardwood floor. Time became countable not by seconds but by the movement of dust motes in the beam of light.

For three hours, I slowly moved around the house, sat, stood, listened. I was feeling the mood of it. Could I live in this brick Cape Cod home mortared together forty-two years ago? Seamed with its sturdy two-by-nines, plastered over its wood-bony frame, and lined with pine-planked wood floors, had the house been treated kindly by its owners? Or had hatred and a lack of charity crept into its helplessly silent walls as relentlessly as termites burrowing into the foundation?

Now empty, the house would never reveal its secrets. Like

a confessional booth with the priest gone, the house would be forever mute about the memories of the former life that had once reverberated through its walls. The birthday screams of delighted children, the muted love-making of parents, the kittens, birds, turtles, and dogs — all had left their memoried imprints in these walls. All the stories were there, recorded forever, if only I could hear them. Like a fortune teller, I now gazed at the walls, my heart listening to its silence.

~

Apartment living, even in solitude, lacked one essential ingredient: nature. With dwellers below and beside me, it was a bustling mini-society. We shared the laundry, the parking lot, the swimming pool. Increasingly, I feared my desire for solitude would get lost, like an unwanted commodity warehoused in a low-cost facility. As lovely as my apartment was, with its sliding glass windows overlooking a wild meadow, I knew I needed to touch the earth. Put my hands on it. I needed a home — with trees and grass, birds and squirrels, gardens and plants.

Now, after months of searching, I had found this house.

I touched the warm wood of the floor, ran my hand across the cool plaster wall, and waited. Nothing but peace came. And so, not knowing any more than that, I bought it.

~

In October, I had a housewarming. Marge tumbled in, clutching a small bag.

"Barbara," she began hurriedly, "I can't stay, but I had to

stop and give you this." She thrust the paper bag into my hands.

I looked inside. One wizened bulb lay in the bottom. Bewildered, I asked, "What is it?"

"It's an iris," Marge exclaimed — as though that explained everything.

"But, why an *iris*?" I asked, determined to ferret out the significance of this gift.

"Barbara," Marge blurted out, ignoring my question, "I kept reading and re-reading the address on your invitation. I couldn't believe it. You bought the house I was born in!"

"You're kidding," I said, momentarily forgetting the bulb. "Marge," I tried to explain the joy welling up in me, "I'm so glad."

The silence of the house had not lied to me. Its history had always been important. Now I knew: love *had* lived here.

"Marge, tell me about the house," I insisted, dragging her into my bedroom. "Who slept here?"

"Oh, that was my sister's and my room." Pointing to the office, she added, "Mom and Dad slept there with the baby."

"How many kids were there?" I asked.

"Seven." Marge laughed, seeing my incredulous face.

She walked upstairs with me, explaining its quirks. The holes in the upstairs bedrooms? "Oh, that was Dad's primitive PA system. He hollered for us through those holes." And the basement electric outlets? "He got a little frustrated with the first floor having so few, so he put ten in the recreation room."

As I listened, I felt quiet joy. I hoped that the walls that had protected her family would sustain me when I felt alone, abandoned, forgotten. I believed this family's presence, their silent echo of love within the walls, would give me courage.

Then, looking back down into the paper bag I still held, I repeated, "Why an iris?"

"Wait till Spring," Marge answered cryptically.

~

In the months ahead, I set two major building blocks of solitude into place.

First, I stopped outside employment. After the separation, I had been fortunate to find work in my profession. I managed a five-million-dollar commercial contract with the U.S. Department of Justice library to run their automated purchasing system. But a lucrative career and the need to integrate solitude into my life had little in common. I carefully examined my finances. I could use investments and writing income to pay my bills. When the contract with Justice ended a year later, I packed up my belongings and went home — to my little brick house — for good. I never sought nine-to-five employment again.

Of all the decisions I would make in the ensuing months, this was clearly the most frightening. I severed myself from financial security and professional status. Now the amputation was complete. I was neither wife nor at-home mother nor career woman.

My second major decision was to simply stop. Stop volunteering. Stop entertaining. Stop going out.

I made a rule. Someone had to find me, want me, ask me. Within a few short months, the telephone stopped ringing. Vast white spaces on my calendar were stark proof I had cut myself off — at least for the moment — from the social world. I trembled. I wanted to be loved, valued, needed — *and* I wanted solitude. I was a living oxymoron.

~

Six months after the housewarming party, I am pulling weeds from the garden bed. I fall into a comfortable rhythm, working my way down slowly through the dead leaves and shriveled chrysanthemums.

It's been a good Winter, I decide.

Over the months, I have leaned heavily into the house to nurture my solitude. The home, mutely and steadfastly, has wrapped me in its beam-and-brick embrace as I have prayed, read, written, and worked within it.

As bitter cold night after night has passed, the house has stood as solid against the howling winds as against my shaking fear. In return, I have watched over it with a vigilant eye — painting walls, replacing the furnace, remodeling the kitchen.

Slowly my solitude has begun to unfurl in the companionable silence of the house. Now, when I open the door to come home, a rush of joy floods through me. I am no longer afraid. The Winter of fear, where dark nights, barren trees, and silence have met, has passed. I have grown to love the stillness of my life.

On this early April day, I am beginning to prepare the garden beds. Gusty Fall winds had hurtled maple leaves from the tree, lodging them against the house. I am working my way from the front of the bed to the back. Nearly finished, I scoop a few more mini-mountains of crusty, dry leaves onto my groundsheet. I scrape away damp leaves, promising the leggy, harvest-orange chrysanthemums underneath that I will properly prune them this year. One more layer remains: decomposing leaves, the embryonic beginnings of new humus. Just like my new life. I push them aside, curious to see if anything is growing, and I burst out laughing.

Dozens of stalks are pushing their way out of the earth.

Irises.

stones

*P*ut the pallets here," I say, pointing to the spot beneath the maple tree. Soon the quarry driver hooks the hoist to a chicken-wired pallet and starts the wench. The first ton of gray-blue Pennsylvania field stone swings out from the truck bed, the hydraulic arm shoving it outward. It hovers over the sidewalk for a moment, then the metal arm pushes it into my yard.

Thirty minutes later, the pallets lie on my lawn. I eye them warily. The first job is to get three tons of stone into my back yard.

My Summer has begun.

~

With the house finally in order, I have turned my attention to the back yard. It looks like an earthen orphan begging for life. Crab grass futilely tries to grow through rock hard clay. Erosion eats away one side of a hill. Vines threaten to overtake the lawn if it is not brutally pruned.

Staring out my kitchen window one day, I make a decision.

Anybody can move dirt. A shovel here, a shovel there. I begin to envision the back yard as a grassy expanse with a stone wall on one side, hedges on the others, and a Zen garden in the middle. The following week, I visit the local quarry.

"I want to build an earthen rock wall in my back yard," I explain. Soon, I have chosen the pallets of rocks I need to begin.

～

Building a wall, I find, is not a task to be hurried through. When finished, my wall will run about fifty feet long and four feet high. Right now, though, the rocks lie strewn across my tiny crab-grassed lawn like neighborhood kids gathering for a game.

I survey the gray-stone players, eyeing their edging, shape, weight, and overall size. If I can coax out each rock's peculiar strength, perhaps this motley crew will fit together into a wall that will withstand snow and ice and heat.

～

I am trying to build silence into my life the same way: taking the misshapen pieces of work, friends, silence, writing, and prayer, and fitting them together into a new way of living. Slowly I begin to test my solitary life. I rock each piece back and forth, checking its solidity. I try praying with a rosary, then with Christian hours of prayer, then with Scripture, sometimes with just a hot cup of tea in my hands. I move and shift the pieces to build a balance between solitude and society in a way that holds firm yet absorbs the storms that invariably come.

Initially, my idea of a life of solitude was as rigid as my

perception of a mortared wall, both meant to be immovably permanent structures. I arranged the hourly foundation of my life into tidy blocks, as though they were perfectly hewn stones. Morning prayer. Spiritual reading. Writing. Working around the house. Evening prayer. All in utter silence. I cemented silence into place with no newspapers, no radio, and little television. Outdoors, I clipped hedges the old-fashioned way, and dragged my hand mower silently across the weeds.

The silence quickly became sterile.

It will be the wall-building that teaches me that strong silence, like strong walls, needs spaces between the definitions to grow vibrant and alive.

~

I start the day early in the morning, bringing out a pitcher of cool water and a glass, setting them on a flat rock. Stone dust and Summer heat make me thirsty. I open the shed to get an orange-handled shovel and pull-on black rubber boots, leaving my garden gloves behind. The stones are as rough as sandpaper, but I can't abide covering my hands. Each stone has a feel to it — a way it settles — that I need to know before I seat it in the wall. I sift through the stones, picking, testing, picking, testing until one feels right. There is something about its shape or weight or feel that attracts me. I pick it up, walk up and down the length of the wall, searching and testing until it snugs into the right spot.

I don't suppose I am the most efficient wall-builder. After placing a few stones, I often sit in the sun on a rock and survey my work, sipping a glass of water. And I rarely work for more than an hour or two a day.

After I place a few layers in a section, I climb on top of a muddy mountain of wet clay dirt and shovel it into the trench between the wall and the dirt bank. After a few scoops, I toss my shovel to one side and stomp the mud into place. Then I re-test my wall to see if the rocks have stood firm.

Sometimes I will be several layers up in one section when I decide there is too much wobble in the wall. If even one rock is placed carelessly, every rock above it becomes more precarious until I have to admit defeat and retrieve the misplaced stone.

The wall keeps a strict accounting.

~

When good friends stop by to ask how "their little hermit" is doing, I invite them to place a rock in my wall. They place their rocks by sight; I now place them by feel. For the first time, I realize silence is teaching me to live by different rules. My solitude often *feels* its way into a hidden reality. No longer bombarded by visual and verbal messages from television, movies, radio, and news, my body is learning inner sight. Often the perfect rock, visually, refuses to conform to the space allotted it. Buried beneath the debris of unused rocks, I'll find a squat, ill-shaped one that, when placed, fits into the wall like a bird in its nest.

A solitary life is something like that. Building the wall is teaching me to relax and trust the unusual, unexpected routes into inner silence. To listen inwardly for the opening to present itself, differently, each day and to surrender to it. Like snugging a rock into an earthen wall.

~

Slowly as the weeks pass, the wall emerges. I am in no hurry. Wall-building, I am finding, needs a measure of silence as its mortar. Stones need the space between them to make them walls.

One day, I ask two men for their price to smooth out the rest of the yard and plant new grass before Fall. After looking at the piles of stone strewn across my yard and the unfinished wall, one of them says, "Well, first we need to finish that wall for you. Three or four hours should do it."

"No," I reply. "Come back in two weeks."

~

So it is that I finally set a deadline. The grass needs planting. The wall needs finishing. I fall into the rhythm of wall-building, my eyes the silent partner to my hands feeling, touching, lifting, placing.

Gradually the stone wall grows to its final height, and the mountain of mud-dirt disappears. At last, it is time for the top layer.

I survey the diminished pile of stone, combing it rock by rock. Some have shallow bellies — good for sitting on, on a hot Summer's day. Others teem with tiny green moss and lichen. Still others have a skinny or wedge-like shape that will gap the space between two larger rocks.

I move and place and shift the stones, reluctant to end the project. But at last, it is done. The final stone is placed. With quiet satisfaction, I know I have found a good home for every rock.

I have learned the silence of inner listening. It is a slow trying of hidden possibilities, I realize. *That same patient work — shifting and re-shifting the pieces of my life — will help me build solitude and society into a strong, soul-filled structure.*

I walk back and forth along my wall with a deep joy, touching it, running my hand slowly along it. At last I come to my favorite rock. It is covered with microscopically tiny lichen, so small they cannot be rubbed off. The belly of that rock looks invitingly concave. I have placed it beneath the shade of my oak tree.

For the first time, I sit upon it, gazing out into the hot Summer afternoon. A gentle breeze ripples through the trees. A sparrow flitters across the yard en route to her nest beneath the eaves. Overhead, the young oak spreads its thin limbs, covering me with its oversized leaves. All is quite still.

I have found a piece of my solitary soul.

writing

$\mathcal{A}$t 9:00 A.M. I carry my cup of coffee into my writing room, formerly the master bedroom in this tiny brick Cape Cod home. Oreo, my canary, almost immediately starts singing. Hannah, the cockatiel, squawks. They, and my greyhound, Penny, are my concession to the need for companionship.

Silence is too harsh, too bleak, to be lived utterly alone, I have found. This realization began one day when I asked myself, *What is this restless urging within me for so much solitude? Is there a bottom to this desire?*

To answer that question, I went away for six weeks to a farmhouse, leaving my already solitary life-style and removing myself further from family, friends, and familiar surroundings. At first, it seemed idyllic. The farmhouse overlooked brown, loamy fields. In the distance, ancient mountains raised their worn-down peaks covered with pines and firs, maples and oaks. Occasionally, an Amish woman would walk up the road, pulling her red Radio Flyer wagon filled with garden harvest and her sleeping infant child.

And beautiful clouds billowed over the hilltops, bringing with them thunderous showers of rain and glowing rainbows.

It seemed a companionable silence.

I had nothing to do. I could read, or not. Cooking only took a few minutes. I had no bills to pay, no writing projects, no deadlines. I was free to experience, for the first time, the fullness of silence. To drink it in, to drown in it, if necessary.

Yet like a milk shake too thick to drink, a little was delicious, a lot became slowly sickening. As day sank into day, a certain heaviness began to build up within me. A dreariness. An unrelenting boredom. And slowly, a creeping fear — a dread that grew darker and darker by the day.

Like a harpy, it rose out of some shadowy grave to terrify me with horrible images of abandonment, friendlessness, lovelessness, loneliness, bleak endlessness, no joy, no peace, no love — no fruit whatsoever.

I realized in a sudden flash of truth, *If I hold this obsession for solitude too tightly, it will destroy me.*

In my possessive stalking of silence, I had sought to capture it, ripping it from its source of holiness. But it refused to be entombed by me. It withdrew so completely I had no way to follow it. When I gave up hope, *then* it illumined itself: in the faint ripple of a breeze, or the note of a bird in the evening; in a butterfly lighting on a flower, or a fallen leaf on the trail. *Open your heart,* it seemed to say, *and wait without waiting. Want without wanting. Hope without hoping. When you open your soul, our silences can become one.*

Dark silence, I learned in the isolated mountain farmhouse, was of my own making. I conjured it out of possessive greed.

Now, when dark silence starts to overtake me, I stop trying

to be heroic. I visit a friend, rent a video, read a novel. I slowly learn that solitude is a process, not a possession. It cannot be hurried or forced. Silence will come into my life at a rate and speed that is safe for making the journey to inner quiet.

~

Taking the slower, safer route to this quiet world, I share my office with Hannah, a beady black-eyed cockatiel who begins her day by stretching her bony, gray neck and emitting raucous, orange-cheeked squawks. Soon, she will be hanging on my wrist as I type, bobbing up and down with my keystrokes, or walking across my desk tossing paper clips on the floor.

In my perfect writer's world, my desk would be as clean as a coffee table, its quiet center occupied by my current manuscript with fresh flowers to one side. In actuality, a five-by-seven photo of a Peruvian monastery with the word *SILENCIO* etched over the arch surveys my messy piles of papers, bills, and unread mail.

The silent act of writing, I have found to my discouragement, creates in its wake a paper trail of chaos.

~

When I first began to record my thoughts, writing had an exotic, exciting quality about it. A romantic thrill, even. It seemed as though I were chasing an elusive lover through a maze. Hidden within its twisted paths was the perfect word, the timeless phrase.

Writing was, for me, a miracle.

I was so afraid of losing it that I resented distractions. A phone call, a child's cry, a dinner-time deadline — I became like a hound who had lost the scent of the fox, baying and yelping in pain over the fragmented memory receding too quickly for me to recapture its word-scent.

I envisioned a perfectly silent world, filled with *time*. If only I had enough of it.

~

I can't pick a precise day or event or moment when my obsession with uninterrupted writing time changed. Perhaps it was a gradual thing, like dawn ripening into a Summer-hot day.

Now, with coffee cup in hand, I come to my office, and time — that measurable master now an obedient dog — lies down on the other side of the door to wait for me to emerge.

The phone may ring, and I will answer it. I may get hungry, and I will eat. But my mind remains still, retentive, listening to inwardness. The interruption does not interrupt. I live in a womb-like world of silent space. The intrusions distort it for a moment, like a child's finger poked into a soft, age-puckered balloon — and then they are gone.

~

Writing, like silence, is the willing stare into imageless inner space, a quiet waiting — like sitting in a garden before the flower has burst through the soil. The seeds and bulbs have been planted in inner quiet, but their exact location and time of bloom is lost.

Time is useless in the writing garden. It is equally useless in the quest for silence. Time-watching, the programmed expectation of desired result, sees the second hand but not the flower emerging.

Like an aged gardener, whose gnarled hands have worked the soil for seasons of suns, writers and solitaries leave time in the tool shed of forgotten necessities. Just as nature requires a spaciousness that ill fits the precision of a second, writing finds its compass in the world of silence — and silence sometimes finds its voice through the writer.

Silence eases words from their heart-hid berth, nudging them out as gently as a mother wills her child to grow in her womb. First a heartbeat, then a tiny nub of a limb, then a hand, then fingers. Slowly a string of words, like the wave of a fetal arm, make their way across the page.

They push themselves out of the portal of silence into the world.

There is a labor to it. A bearing down hard on the silence. A pushing. A time in the writing process when a piece is in the birth canal. It will emerge — that at last has become certain. But will it be alive? *Could* it be alive if it were not for silence?

Not even the writer knows.

When I close the door to my office, the answer, tilled into the inked paper of the manuscript now on my desk, lies hidden in the unclockable silence of eternal time.

the candle

When I am anxious and feeling off-center, I often climb my stairs to the second floor, seeking the slope-roofed, green room. Its walls are perhaps a bit too green. The paint, when purchased, promised to be a delicate hint of mellowed lime. When I rolled the first swath of it onto the wall, it metamorphosed from delicate to bold, from a hint to a splash. Standing on a tarp-covered floor with half the can spilled into my paint pan, I had been horrified. This was where I intended to meditate and refresh myself! But the walls looked more leap-frog-green than the "mist" the can promised. I wondered, *How will I ever quiet myself in this color?*

Silence, I have found, opens its mysteries only when I agree to listen. A hard task. Even after all these years, I hesitate to slip so vulnerably into its presence. I prefer silence in the courtyards of my own ego'd life — not silence in its own court. In this green room, I am all too likely to meet it at a depth that still mystifies and alarms me.

I suspect this green-walled mother of silence well knows

my reluctance, for it welcomes me like a wayward child coming home. Perhaps I need its no-nonsense tone, for every time I enter the room, I find its strong, cooling color stops me in my tracks and propels me into silence. I am wrapped in its lush, limed embrace.

～

I pull open the drawer of my mother's old mahogany table and take out the lighter, a gift from my daughter Lisa. She had used it at a rock concert. Swaying ecstatically to the rock group's hits, her lighter had been one tiny torch in a sea of teen-held, bobbing BICs.

Now I light my prayer candle with it. I smile, remembering the concert. That evening, I had uttered the mother's mantra that this, too, might pass. As the numbing blast of decibeled music, so atonal to my ears, crashed over us, it had become the Gregorian-updated chant beneath which I sank into my own muted world.

I affectionately take her gift and hold its flame against the wick until my prayer room kindles into light.

In the procession of candles that have lit this room, tonight's grocery-store taper is perhaps the most lowly. It surrenders itself in unassuming, dripless-purple acceptance to my need for illumined prayer.

～

When I first began my journey into silence, I believed that I needed a firm foundation to support a solitary lifestyle. To that end, I had bought a house that radiated love and established a daily routine of prayer, reading, writing, and work. Most importantly, I had created a center where silence could become a sacramental presence in my life.

I remember walking back and forth between the two up-stairs bedrooms, wondering which would become that focal point — a room used for no other purpose than silence. I expected it to become the most sacred place in my home.

Eventually I picked the smaller room and slowly allowed it to define itself. I kept it simple: An unused birch cabinet lay flat beneath one eave. A cross, the sign of my faith, swung from a piece of nylon fishing line. Two heavy pots of rich black soil nurtured a profusion of plants. A wood-armed chair became my sitting place. And on the birch wood stood one solitary candle.

Every night, I mounted the stairs for an hour of prayer. Solitude, I believed, was something to be cemented into place by a regimented lifestyle.

Living alone gradually taught me otherwise.

Building the wall. Meeting the dark side of silence. Seeing the eventual sterility of forcing solitude into rigid structures. Per-haps the silent room itself taught me.

However it happened, I began to carry the presence of that room, the pulse of silence, within my heart. Wherever I was — at home or abroad — I could feel its strong current. Outwardly, to my friends, I seemed *less* solitary. I enjoyed their company outra-geously, laughing sometimes until tears rolled down my cheeks. Unbeknownst to them, I continued to feel silent, an interior silence within my soul.

I was slowly becoming another contradiction — the sociable hermit.

The upstairs room had become more like a mother to be turned to when I felt I needed a deep physical sense of quiet. For some strange reason, the room has always had the effect of drawing me down to the hidden needs of my soul.

~

On this Winter night, the air is quite still. I sink contentedly into the peach-upholstered chair, wrapping myself in a skin-soft, purple shawl. The flame begins to burn, gaining a confident shape. The room seems to seduce the light from its static, waxen wick until the flame surrenders, glowing warm into the timeless silence of the walls. Once two boys shared a bedroom here, a circular Orioles baseball sticker permanently adhered to their bedroom door. Then it became a room of books. Now it is a prayer room. The room amiably accepts our intrusions, our interpretations, paint, door stickers.

I sit in the chair and, like a woman before her confessor, I find my feelings emerging from their secret hiding places — places they have cowered all day long. Ignoring me, they begin to commune with the silence of the green room illumined by the single candle. It requires no coaxing on my part, no uttered mantra or prayer beads. No pleading with the divine.

Time is not measured in this room by minutes and seconds. It is measured by change.

My heart softens, sighs, and settles back into itself.

I glance at candle. Perhaps an inch of tapered silence was required to melt the daily concerns from my heart this evening.

Molten wax has etched a path down its long slender back. I stand up, quietly say a good-bye prayer, stoop over the candle, and puff.

The flame flickers, falters, fades to a glow, releasing its smoke-slow tracks into the night.

the candle

127

PART IV: LIVING IN SILENCE

The night of total calm
before the rising winds of dawn,
the music of a silence,
the sounding solitude,
the supper that renews our love.

— "Spiritual Canticle," St. John of the Cross

even now

*M*e as I was
long long ago
even then
thinking dreaming
alone
even then.

Running my hands through nature
swinging on grass
with fireflies and caterpillars
even then.

I one'd with life
I alone

Now
after marriage
divorce
children
leaving

It is not so different.

I run my hands through nature
swinging on grass
with fireflies and caterpillars

even now.

dawn

Sleep, the dark, warm shadow that has smoothly covered me all night long, begins a slow, mute retreat. A languorous ebbing away, tiding out until I find myself beached on the cold sands of morning.

It is still dark outside. My neighbor's security light invades my privacy blinds, casting lined silhouettes on the far wall. I lie there wishing it were moonlight and not a halogen bulb etching the dreamy patterns.

Overhead, the fan slaps its blades against the damp morning air, sending moist waves of it over my now awake skin. *Another sultry August day.* I unwrap my body from its pillow nest and swing my bare feet onto the wood floor, being careful not to wake my greyhound.

I am a morning person, one who delights in the birth of day.

I slip past my closed office door, happy to ignore the work waiting inside, and go to the kitchen to start the morning coffee.

The two-decker, stainless-steel coffee pot sits upended on the drain board. *Dad's coffee pot, the one encrusted with years of never-washed crud until I inherited it.* I silently chuckle as I assemble it, ladling four scoops into its basket.

Picking up my metal pitcher, I walk to the water dispenser. Water from Bear Springs begins a cascade into its silvery bowels. I close my eyes, half asleep. Glub. I peer into the dark unmarked pitcher. Glub. I am waiting for a certain tone.

Glub. I let go of the hot water lever.

I pour the boiling water into the upper compartment. Putting on the lid, I turn to leave. *It will take about five minutes.* The living room is still deep in shadows. I pull the cord on the pink, papery, honeycombed blind. It soundlessly glides up. Cars sit at silent sentinel on the street. Trees, too oppressed by the heat to move, smother the community in heavy, green stillness. I know it will be another day of soupy silence, simmering like a long-cooking stew in the murky broth of Summer.

I sit in my mother's chair, a Queen Anne of questionable history, and stretch out my long, bare legs to wait. In the kitchen the steady drip of the water seeps through the coffee grounds into the pot below.

From this chair by the window, I have watched the seasons pass by like models on a runway. Fall dresses for success. The Autumn-colored beauty kisses and waves from the runway like a model who already knows she has a better contract elsewhere. Winter, clothed in darkness so black even the trees are invisible, haunts the runway like an aging diva uttering the last crystalline note in an opera. Spring flounces by with the insouciance of a teasing stripper trailing her luscious scented silence. And Summer?

The old runway queen, whisker-cheeked and heavy, sits like a Buddha on her throne, pouring thick, humid night air through the sieve of her fat fingers into another drip-grind dawn.

I prefer Winter, I decide, feeling sweat bead on my upper lip . . .

~

Now dressed, I unlock the door, open it, and step into the early morning. A luscious wetness wraps itself around me like the feel of cool silk against bare skin. *I won't need my jacket,* I decide.

I reach into the hall closet and retrieve the blue, retractable leash hanging on a hook. Penny stretches her lean greyhound body into the wood of the floor. When she rises, I clip her worn collar into its steel clasp, and we head out. She takes a flying leap off the front steps effortlessly, the twenty-five-foot cord rapidly unwinding from the casing held in my hand.

We head uphill, beneath the overhanging branches of the magnolia tree, its gray-barked, limb-fingers carrying platters of dark-leaf shade throughout the Summer. "There are good times and bad times," my neighbor Ken once explained when I caught him sweeping rotting Spring blossoms from his sidewalk.

Muffie, nine gray-black pounds of silently majestic Lhasa apso fur, sits sphinx-like in front of Laura's house. Only when my eighty-five-pound greyhound bounds up the hill to nuzzle her does she relinquish her post, accompanying us for the next hundred yards or so.

I round the corner, clipping on the leash lock as a protection against an unexpected car, and breathe in the fragrant morning silence. Soon commuters, cars, and children will shatter its stillness with doors slamming, engines starting, shouts, and sleepy laughter — determined to wrest day from dawn into a nine-to-five submission.

But now it is only 6:30 in the morning.

At the edge of the park, I release the catch on Penny's leash. She surveys the ground, her nose ferreting out prior visitors. It isn't long before she arches her back.

The urgent needs of nature now taken care of, we begin our leisurely stroll along the shady road circling the grounds. I scan the acre or so for rabbits or deer. Seeing none, I unhook Penny, nudging her forward. She bounds past me, heading toward the Blessed Mary statue, thinking perhaps it is prey. I keep an eye on her.

She stops, sniffs a moist patch of leaves, turns, and seeing me, comes sailing back, ears flat, lean body stretching into the air, thoroughbred-thin legs airborne. In seconds, she comes to a panting halt beside me, and I hook her again to the leash.

We saunter down to the creek. Penny eyes the water rolling past. She cautiously negotiates the steep bank and soon is standing in the middle, lapping rock-tumbled water as it flows between her bony legs.

By afternoon, the neighborhood kids will be tossing balls or biking in the park. They will surround Penny, stroking her head, peering at her racetrack tattoos and asking if they can ride her. Penny will patiently accept their homage until they tire and leave.

But now, we begin our walk home. As we walk uphill, I hold my gaze on the corner-street maple, surely the neighborhood matriarch. I turn the corner, careful not to step on her majestic old roots that have slowly moved the level sidewalk aside. Past Norma's gardens filled with boxwood and peonies. Past the basketball hoop in the new cement driveway. We turn the last corner. Soon parents will be dropping toddlers off next door; and Leah, her blond hair billowing, will walk her brindle-colored greyhound.

A car starts a descent down the hill. The neighbor across the street opens his door to retrieve the newspaper. I take one last look into the morning sky already beginning to sink beneath the hot dreary wetness of a humid day, then turn to go inside.

The silence of dawn is over. I feel it ebbing away as I near the front door. My to-do list starts to spill into its stillness: *Write the column. Call the insurance company. Sweep the floors. Mow . . .*

The flow of my day begins.

the broom

*T*oday I broom-sweep the floor. I use one of those soft-bristle push brooms that catches dustballs and pushes leaves and dirt into tidy piles. It is as silent as the house itself.

I start in the bedroom — the tiniest room on the first floor. I know all the favorite hiding places for dustballs now — beneath the bed, behind the door. The tiny piles emerge from hiding, gently pried from their dens by the soft, gray-whiskered broom.

One mound safely stowed in a pick-up spot in the living room, I open the door to my office — always a disheartening experience. Unlike dust balls, bird feathers are hostile to brooms. They float when they should lay, flutter when they should flop; they refuse to be moved in any direction but upward or into unreachable corners. The results are always unsatisfactory. I have never made friends with the by-products of my birds. The billowing mess of dust and feathers, the small part that the broom can conquer, reluctantly joins the pick-up pile. In the corner of my eye, I can see feathers swirling upward, caught in the vortex of air left by the final thrust of my broom.

The high point of sweeping — if there can be such a thing — is restoring the wood floors in the living room to barefoot-smooth cleanliness. The wood seems to open itself like a woman to love. Nothing is concealed, nothing hidden. I gently draw the broom across the entryway, carefully scooping the corners, trimming beneath the sofa pleats, happy with the yield of accumulated signs of life in this room. The white-tile coffee table is shoved to one side, and I draw long clean strokes down the width of the room. I pull my mother's old Queen Anne chair away from the wall. I nudge the dust clinging to its claw-balled feet out and sweep up the fallen leaves from the orange tree behind it. A quick swoop beneath a glass table under the window, and the floor is almost clean.

All that remains is the rocker. In the two years it has sat there, rocking away, grit beneath its legs has worn through the varnished floor, leaving behind a massive network of scratches. Like an anxious mother, I love both the rocker and the floor but wish they got along better with each other. I slide the rocker from its corner and sweep up the latest accumulation of grit. The living room is finished.

I feel the joy of wood-warm silence most in this room.

The gate-leg mahogany dining room table truculently awaits the banging of my broom pole against its tightly nested legs. I navigate beneath it, cornering lost, shriveled-up peas and nuggets of dog food thrown by Penny's dinnertime eating frenzy. The sweeping is now complete. Like a farmer examining the harvest, I measure my joy by the size of the pick-up piles.

I rummage through the detergents and bottles beneath the sink and snake out the red dust pan from its hiding place. Retracing my steps, I stop at each pile, sweeping it neatly with a small duster into the red bin. Carrying my precariously balanced dustball treasure outside, I flip the pan off the side of the brick porch watching the dust billow down into the garden bed below.

At last, I lean against the broom pole, surveying the clean floor, grateful for the everyday silence of routine.

I take off my shoes. The silent wood feels good against my bare feet. I bend over to touch it, running my hand across its grained forty-four-year-old body. It is silken smooth beneath my touch. *This is how a woman feels after she has been caressed by her lover,* I reminisce. *It is the warm silence of unspoken love.*

Quietly, I put away the broom. When silence has entered, it is best to rest in the center of it. Even thought destroys the afterglow of ordinary silence.

chopping broccoli

*L*ate Sunday morning, after church, I drive to the organic produce market. The sub-sized carts are stacked in neat, metallic order. I wheel one small basket over to the vegetables.

In this mom-and-pop store, vegetables are the royal court. They rule over the flour bins and tofu, the cereal boxes and unrefined virgin oils. The owner obviously loves them. They are laid out, color by color, as though in a formal garden.

The dark rhododendron-colored broccoli, crisp beneath early morning moisture, hovers near the clumps of carrots with their fairy-haired tops still intact. The red-tinged leaf lettuce frames hairy white parsnips. Dark humus still clings to plump white mushrooms. Even the dull green kale offers up a crisp bob of curled leaves as a subtle accent for the glossy, yellow-skinned zucchini.

Sometimes I come into the store glancing at my watch. *I just need two or three vegetables for the soup. Kale, potatoes, maybe a leek.* I have intentions, plans, a purpose. Then my eye encounters the vegetable court — and all is lost. They brook no frenzy or callousness. They gaze at me silently forbidding haste.

Today I park my cart next to the yams. Slowly I walk from one end of the vibrant display to the other. In my mind's eye is my empty pot. Every Sunday, I prepare a new cauldron of soup. Each different. Never a recipe. Rather, a feel for the week — a wondering of how my body is reaching out into the first touches of Spring, or hailing the Fall. Enduring the Summer, or nestling under for the Winter.

I give my body time, stopping before each vegetable. It is lost in remembering the taste, the smell, the touch. I can feel the hard sturdiness of the kale bunched beneath my fingers as I slice through it. The easy glide of the knife severing the yellow squash in two. The sweet, juicy, succulent taste of a raw mushroom.

I continue down the aisle. The sand-gritty, green-stalked leek, the arrogantly large red-skinned yam, the dark earthy burdock root all beckon.

Today I pick broccoli, two white-skinned potatoes, one leek, two yellow squash, and a fresh bundle of kale. I hover over the first ears of yellow corn from Florida. *Too expensive,* I decide. I walk away. I walk back. *One. Just one.* The first sign of Spring.

I gaze at my choices now lying in the seat of my cart. I roll it past the plastic bag dispenser. I never have the desire to subject the vegetables, regal even in submission, to polyethylene.

At the check-out counter, I pick each one, still cool to my touch, out of the cart and lay it on the black conveyer belt. The checker touches the pedal, and the belt begins to move. The vegetables collide into one another, rolling down the black alley onto a weighing machine. The white potatoes slide into the dark green broccoli. The leek leans up against the single spectacularly yellow ear of corn.

A quiet anticipation begins to grow inside me. I feel my body slowing. Sliding imperceptibly into a sabbath of silence.

"$5.46, please."

~

I lift each vegetable out of the paper bag and place it gently next to the cutting area. My wooden chopping board is not much to look at. It has aging red and yellow flowers painted on it, like a Mennonite stencil pattern on the side of a barn. It must have cost all of three dollars years ago. On the cutting side, you can see the seams of three boards glued together.

Sometimes I think I'd love to have a solid oak cutting board. The warm rich feel of wood beneath my fingers. Broad enough to push each pile of colored chopped vegetables to one side. This is a scrawny board. But I know its feel. I am so much it; it is so much me.

I have one knife with a flat broad blade. My fingers have wrapped around its handle for years, memories of a hundred odors pushed into its worn wood. The Japanese assure me it will last forever. The thought contents me.

I pick up the broccoli and lay it flat upon the board, like an emerald queen beneath the guillotine. I push the blade against the base of the flowerets and slice them off. The stalk looks naked, vulnerable, its beauty shorn off so quickly. I slice it down the middle. I lay each half on its chlorophyll flat belly and cut it again. With a rolling rhythm, I chop the quarters into chunks.

My children once told me I'm a fast cutter. "There is a rhythm to it," I replied. "Like a heartbeat."

Laying a carrot down, I begin to move my blade through it. Time is stretching out slowly now. I cut into the space between the seconds. Silent time, I call it. Unmeasured. Unclocked. And the vegetable is willing. I suppose.

Each vegetable is scooped up in my hands and quietly laid into the large metal pot. Layer upon layer. Broccoli. Squash. Potato. Leek. Kale. Corn.

I slowly pour water over them, turn on the gas flame, and dry my hands. The pot begins to simmer.

Every soup is different. Sometimes Penny will refuse to eat her dry dog food, waiting until the soup is done. She'll stand in the kitchen, taking up what little room remains, and stretch. Her legs slide forward and down. Her brown-fur shoulders hover tantalizing inches above the floor. She yawns. When she rises, she gives a shake as though knowing this quiet interlude, the slow time of a Sunday afternoon, is over.

When the soup is done, I pour two portions. One for me, one for her. We wait for it to cool. I rinse the wooden ladle beneath running water and place it in the stone bowl by the stove. There it will stay all week, ladling, resting, ladling, resting till the pot is empty.

Whoever comes to visit that week receives a bowl of soup, simmered in Sunday silence.

the flower

I pull open the old wooded door of the Blue Iris flower shop and step out of the bitter Winter cold into the oriental-carpeted room filled with flowers. The cut roses and colorful carnations are still in their large, white buckets filled with water, waiting the florist's selection. Behind them, in the glassed refrigerator units, are some of the more exotic flowers, like the deep purple-blue iris, long-stem roses, and white-petaled mums. The room is filled with the green fragrance of flowers still tightly budded in expectation of tomorrow's bloom.

On the old wood counters, candles rise out of dry flowered bouquets, and tiny copper kettles show clusters of bright silk red arrangements. The walls are hung with bowed wreathes. Vases of silk flowers and containers of dried roses hover in the corners.

Whenever I enter this store, surrounded by the fragrance of the flowers, I sink into gentling silence. Everything in me slows. The afternoon errands are not yet done, the dinner not cooked.

Here, my hustling ceases. It seems that even time itself bows to the bouquets, listening to their secrets.

Once a week, I, too, come to pay court. I come to buy a single flower.

~

I found the vase for my flower in a small town near the Chesapeake Bay. One day, I walked into a gift shop on the main street. In the center of the room stood a table holding, among other things, a single pink carnation floating in an inverted pyramid of glass. In this crystalline pond, the flower found the perfect center of its glassed world.

I stood there admiring it, paralyzed by its beauty. I turned to leave. I had no plans for purchasing a vase that day.

I was perhaps fifty feet away from the store when I turned back, returned, and bought it.

The woman who owned the shop lifted the glass prism from the table. The carnation began to rock gently to and fro as she gently carried it into the back room. She washed and dried the triangular sides of the vase, and carefully wrapped it for me. On the top of the tissue, she placed the one cut carnation. It spread its pink petals moistly out. I gazed in at it, overjoyed. Then the lid to the box was sealed.

"It comes with a frog," the woman explained.

I remembered my mother's collection. Circular and rectangular metal bases with needle teeth sticking up to skewer flowers securely in place. Such a funny name: "Frog."

~

I carried the box into the kitchen and placed it on the green counter top. Gently, I removed the carnation, still vibrant with life. Then I carefully lifted the vase out of its tissued cradle. I filled it with water and placed the carnation back in its bath. The flower slowly bobbed from one side to another as I carried it to the coffee table and placed it on a square of Finnish linen-thread lace. Slowly the water began to still. I left the two, the vase and the flower, to acquaint themselves again and returned to the kitchen to unpack groceries. When I returned, the flower was floating once again in the perfect center of its triangular world.

~

"Could I have a mum today?" I ask the woman. It is the Saturday before Christmas. The delivery van outside is loaded with poinsettias, and the brown-haired woman is red-cheeked from carrying their cardboard trays to the truck.

She opens the door to the refrigerator, and together we gaze at each of the three mums in their chilled bucket of water. We agree that the one most tightly petaled is the freshest. She plucks it from the water and places it on the narrow counter, turning to gather tissue to wrap it in.

I think I love the ceremony of wrapping as much as the flower selection.

"Do you want some baby's breath?" she asks. When I assent, she disappears into the other small room to lean over another bucket filled with the tiny, snow-fleck-sized blossoms. She returns carrying a large cluster and places them beside the mum.

The wrapping tissue contains vibrant purple pansies against a forest green background. She folds the flowers into their tissued nest and ties a pink ribbon around them, flourishing it into a bow.

"That will be $1.05," she announces.

It is here that I am most humbled. I have stepped out of my errand-filled world into a timeless garden filled with slow, delicate movement, and for such richness . . .

I gaze down at my flower nestled in tissue and gratefully place my dollar and nickel in her hand. "Thank you," I say, unable to explain what it means to me or how much I will love to watch the white mum slowly unfold its petals as the week goes by.

~

I cut the long, green stem with my old kitchen scissors and quickly place it on the frog. The mum has such round beauty, I can't quite bear to conceal any of its charm in water. I place tiny snippets of baby's breath around it so it seems to soar above the water, suspended above a world of falling snow.

When evening turns into night and dewed dusk drapes the day, I come to rest for a while before the flower. There is mystery here that I tremble to touch. An end to all knowing. A hope held in a single vibrant blossom. I follow its steadfast petaled gaze into the silken center of silence.

evening

I sleep in the tiniest room in the house. For a long time, my bed mattress sat on a metal frame nailed to unpainted four-by-four blocks of wood. Sleep, in my mind, did not need embellishment. Then one day, a leg worked its way loose at 2:00 in the morning, and I fell on the floor.

The next day I bought a real bed, a simple pine-doweled bed.

It took me three days to put its Swedish-built pieces together. I'd sit on the bare pine wood floor reading and re-reading the instructions. I'd pick up a likely looking bolt, lace it through a hole juxtaposing two pieces of the frame, and the whole thing would crash down around me. After several tries, I'd give up, preferring to sleep on the sofa. Eventually, I found a way to cantilever the four major pieces simultaneously while inserting the five-inch bolts. After that, the bolts, washers, braces, and slats, though tedious, were a cinch.

Once built, I slid the bed into the corner between two windows, and there it has sat since.

~

As though anticipating the bed's arrival, I had bought an Amish hand-stitched quilt the year before. It was, I suppose, a dowry investment in my own future. I could foresee that one day it would adorn a new bed.

I found it in a tiny Pennsylvania Dutch country store. Behind counter-top Amish memorabilia of cookbooks, postcards, and dolls, it hung tightly squeezed among other quilts on a wall-mounted rack, a dusky tiny-rose-flowered blue quilt with large white-pointed petals sewn onto it. The tag safety-pinned to its edge read, "*DAHLIA. One of the favorite patterns of the area. Over 400 hours to complete. $398.*"

On my budget, $398 could buy a whole bed.

I gently touched the elegantly raised, four-pointed flowers hand-cut and sewn by Elsie May. Her tiny stitches left their smaller-than-quarter-inch tracks down the sides of the flowers and up and down the fabric pieces. This Amish grandmother, the store owner proclaimed, was one of the finest quilters in the area. I could see her needle-callused, eighty-year-old fingers flying up and down the blue and rose-colored pieces framing the luscious dahlia petals on a cold Winter night — their pattern alone promising Spring.

You don't need it, I sternly told myself. It was a wasted argument.

That evening, the quilt lay on my bed, a white-petaled virgin folded open.

~

All day the bedroom slumbers in shadows waiting for the late afternoon brilliance of the sun. At last, its rays filter through the room's tiny, slat-blinded windows casting a sunny glow on the slumbering dahlias below. It is the first sign that night is coming.

During the day, I often pass the room, its silent suggestion of slumber beckoning me as I walk between office, basement, and bathroom. Not even the living room escapes its gentle vigilance. When I finally sit quietly in the Queen Anne's chair by the window at day's end, I have only to look up to see the dalhia'd bed.

I love the evening with its slowed pace and quietness. I am always reluctant to leave it — even for sleep. Night is the time I come into myself without words or thoughts. It is here, surprisingly, that I will sometimes let gentle traces of sound into my silent world. Music from a CD will stir the air. Evening birds chirp through an open window. Words from a book resonate as though spoken. But eventually the music ends, the birds go to sleep, and the book lies, unread, in my lap. I rest with a cup of tea, and a thought or two. Silence settles in undisturbed.

As evening sinks into night and the hours begin to pile too high upon my day-wearied body, I close the book or put the cup of tea down. I turn off the light, lock the doors, lower the last blinds of the day, and walk to the bedroom.

Penny is already asleep on the wood floor between my dresser and closet. I step back and forth over her, folding and hanging my clothes, and slip into a nightshirt. I pause for a moment to look up, as I do every night, at the framed black-and-white photograph over the dresser. A Salvadoran woman my age looks down on her seventh child, a daughter born under a parish stairwell to keep her safe from the war raging outside. I follow her quiet,

Buddha-like gaze toward the child, who appears to be about three years old. Dressed in white, the girl stands motionless by her mother, one hand splayed on her mother's knee while she gazes at some unseen distant object. Her dark child-eyes, warm and contenting, hold my silent, unresolved interest in her.

I turn, fold the dahlia-petaled quilt into a pleated pile at the foot of the bed, and draw down the age-softened sheet. I settle the pillows into their nocturnal stations and sit on the bed's edge. My muscles, weary from their day's work, sink with silent celebration into the mattress's soft embrace. I am, at last, attending to their exhaustion. I stretch like a cat about to own its territorial bed, my toes touching one end, my fingers the other. I relinquish myself to the elusive silence of night.

Overhead, the ceiling fan makes its slow, rhythmic blade-pole dance over my weary body. Outside, my neighbor is blowing soft sorrowful notes into the humid night with his saxophone. They lullaby me to sleep.

silent endings

I have let go of noise
the whirring machines and nightly news
slipping into a sweet sweet night
of silence.

past the familiar portals
past the places I once played
letting go the grip
of my secure moorings

to a down, down inward falling
Oh, most gentle fall!
where all my unendings
meet in one certainty:

Silence is naught but Love.

EPILOGUE

In deepest solitude
I found the narrow way:
a secret giving such release
that I was stunned and stammering
rising above all science.

— "I Came into the Unknowing," St. John of the Cross

ABOUT THE AUTHOR

Barbara Erakko Taylor began her career as a librarian, moved into automated information systems design, and designed and installed a system used by President Carter to track press releases. This information system was later adopted by several government agencies and Fortune 500 companies.

Her writing career has included everything from White House training manuals and an anecdotal history book on electric cars, to poetry, freelance articles, and columns. She has been a columnist for *Catholic Review* since 1992 and has traveled to El Salvador, Nicaragua, and Honduras on various delegations. She is also active in prison ministry and teaches creative writing.

She has led a contemplative life style for nearly twenty years.

Innisfree
Press, Inc.

*A call to the
deep heart's core*